May you have a Blessed Easter!

Love & blessings,
Gayle

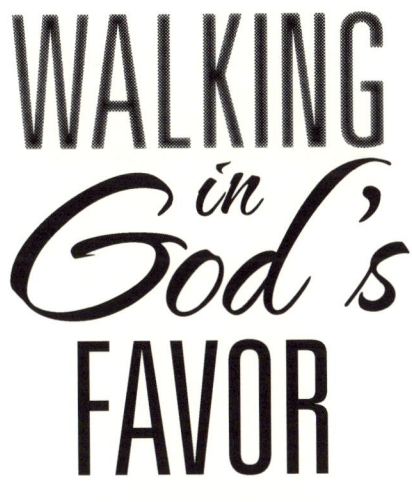

A Daily Devotional

Christina Marie Hollensbe

WestBow Press
A DIVISION OF THOMAS NELSON
& ZONDERVAN

Copyright © 2017 Christina Marie Hollensbe.

All rights reserved. No part of this book may be used or reproduced by any means, graphic, electronic, or mechanical, including photocopying, recording, taping or by any information storage retrieval system without the written permission of the author except in the case of brief quotations embodied in critical articles and reviews.

This book is a work of non-fiction. Unless otherwise noted, the author and the publisher make no explicit guarantees as to the accuracy of the information contained in this book and in some cases, names of people and places have been altered to protect their privacy.

WestBow Press books may be ordered through booksellers or by contacting:

WestBow Press
A Division of Thomas Nelson & Zondervan
1663 Liberty Drive
Bloomington, IN 47403
www.westbowpress.com
1 (866) 928-1240

Because of the dynamic nature of the Internet, any web addresses or links contained in this book may have changed since publication and may no longer be valid. The views expressed in this work are solely those of the author and do not necessarily reflect the views of the publisher, and the publisher hereby disclaims any responsibility for them.

Any people depicted in stock imagery provided by Thinkstock are models, and such images are being used for illustrative purposes only. Certain stock imagery © Thinkstock.

ISBN: 978-1-5127-6018-7 (sc)
ISBN: 978-1-5127-6019-4 (hc)
ISBN: 978-1-5127-6017-0 (e)

Library of Congress Control Number: 2016916885

Print information available on the last page.

WestBow Press rev. date: 01/09/2017

Scripture quotations from THE MESSAGE. Copyright © by Eugene H. Peterson 1993, 1994, 1995, 1996, 2000, 2001, 2002. Used by permission of NavPress. All rights reserved. Represented by Tyndale House Publishers, Inc.

Scripture quotations marked (ERV) are taken from the HOLY BIBLE: EASY-TO-READ VERSION © 2001 by World Bible Translation Center, Inc. and used by permission

Scripture quotations taken from the Amplified® Bible (AMPC), Copyright © 1954, 1958, 1962, 1964, 1965, 1987 by The Lockman Foundation Used by permission. www.Lockman.org

Scripture quotations marked (TLB) are taken from The Living Bible copyright © 1971. Used by permission of Tyndale House Publishers, Inc., Carol Stream, Illinois 60188. All rights reserved.

Scripture quotations marked (NIV) are taken from the Holy Bible, New International Version®, NIV®. Copyright © 1973, 1978, 1984, 2011 by Biblica, Inc.™ Used by permission of Zondervan. All rights reserved worldwide. www.zondervan.com The "NIV" and "New International Version" are trademarks registered in the United States Patent and Trademark Office by Biblica, Inc.™

Scripture taken from the New King James Version®. Copyright © 1982 by Thomas Nelson. Used by permission. All rights reserved.

Scripture quotations marked (GNT) are from the Good News Translation in Today's English Version- Second Edition Copyright © 1992 by American Bible Society. Used by Permission.

Scripture quotations taken from the New American Standard Bible® (NASB), Copyright © 1960, 1962, 1963, 1968, 1971, 1972, 1973, 1975, 1977, 1995 by The Lockman Foundation Used by permission. www.Lockman.org

Scripture is taken from GOD'S WORD®, © 1995 God's Word to the Nations. Used by permission of Baker Publishing Group.

Contents

Acknowledgements xiii
Introduction xv

He is the God that Sees You 1
Lay Down Like the Lion 5
The Homeless Man 9
Bondage Breaker 12
What Can I Expect from God? 14
You are Loved 17
The .05 Cent Bubble Gum 19
Life is Beautiful 21
The Cleft of the Rock 23
Keeping Up With Appearances 25
God's Grace 27
Drowning in His Presence 31
Comparison, the Thief of Contentment 33
Fingerprints of God 35
Wrestling in the Spirit 37
Light In A Dark World 39
A Treacherous Heart 41
These Hands 45
Who Shall You Follow? 48
Praises of the Heart 50
Faith Like a Child 53
Pride and Prejudice 55

True Success	57
Dealing with Controlling People	59
Spiritual Bullies	61
The Leprous Man	63
The Stolen Seed	67
Toxic Relationships	69
Fool's Gold	71
Prosper Even as Your Soul Prospers	73
Law vs Grace	75
Gathering with the Brethren	77
Bearing Good Fruit	79
Celebrate	81
God vs Idols	83
New Covenant	85
Out of the Cage of Religion	87
Sanctified for a Purpose	89
Spiritual Slumber	90
Fruit Inspectors	92
Earthly Riches	94
Manipulation	96
Wisdom Beyond Years	98
Setting Up a Monument	100
Radical Christianity	102
Choosing Love Over Fear	104
Why We Need the Holy Spirit	106
Walking in a Spirit of Excellence	108
The Gift of Forgiveness	110
Assumptions of the Accuser	112
Refraining from Lying Lips	114

A Heart of Deception	116
Not Forsaken	118
A Culture Enticed by Sexual Impurity	120
The Silent Killer	122
God's Justice	124
Freedom From Addiction	126
Fighting Well	129
Stewarding Spiritual Gifts	131
Reconciliation	133
Flattering Titles	135
Healing Shame	137
Renewed Strength	139
For the Working Class	141
Dealing with Emotions	143
It's A New Season	145
Principles of Marriage	149
The Samaritan Woman	150
A Life of Singleness, Not Loneliness	152
A Fraudulent Faith	154
Be Confident in Who God has Created You to Be	156
Scribes and Pharisees	158
Saved Lives, Changed Lives	160
Making Assumptions	162
Trust, Such a Complicated Ordeal	164
Arise and Shine	166
Trusting God Through Brokenheartedness	168
The Empty Tomb	170
Does God Still Heal?	172
A Heart of Courage	174

Feminist?..176

Fatherless Generation 178

Leadership Roles and Responsibilities..................................... 180

Hope Through Persecution 182

The Double-Minded Man.. 184

Do Good to Please God 186

Drunkenness and Gluttony Leads to Poverty 188

Obedience Rewarded 190

Undeserved Mercy and Grace 192

A Submitted Heart...194

Spiritual Parenting 196

Man's Discipline vs God's Discipline.......................................198

Steady My Heart.. 200

Flesh vs Spirit.. 202

Worship the Creator, not His Creation................................... 204

God Loves Those that Struggle with Their Sexuality Too 206

He Will Turn it All Around 208

Incased by Grace..210

The Ultimate Love Story...212

The Problem with the Message of Prosperity.........................214

Don't Take the Master's Body to a Brothel 216

Walk on Water...218

A Call to Unworldliness 220

Against All Odds 222

Resurrection Day 224

Letting Go of the Past 226

Your Joy is Coming... 228

The Heart-Shattered Life 230

When Evil Prevails.. 232

Cross-Gender Boundaries 234
Be Set Free 236
Are You Running the Right Race?... 239
The Time is Ripe for a Miracle 241
Kicking Over the Money Tables.. 243
Mending Broken Hearts... 247

Acknowledgements

First and foremost I would like to thank God. Several years ago, He gave me a vision where my hand was writing so fast, my mind couldn't keep up. Never in my wildest dreams would I have envisioned all that God would do through my writings... putting pen to paper while being inspired by Him. I now realize what an honor, privilege, and gift it is to be able to spend my days writing.

To my mother, Rachel Koch: Thank you mom for the long conversations, for telling me you are proud of me, for encouraging me in my God-given destiny, and most importantly, for praying for me. Thank you for all the love and support you have shown me. I love you.

To my husband, John Hollensbe: Thank you for all your love and support. You do so much and expect very little in return. Thank you for believing God in me. I am so thankful that God gave me you and that I have you in my life. Thank you for making me laugh and teaching me that it's okay to be silly. Our life has been quite an adventure and I look forward to sharing many more adventures with you. You are my Best Friend and I love doing life with you. Love you so much!

To my brothers, Luis & Noe Garcia: I love you guys very much. You both have always made me feel as if you were very proud that I was your big sister. I love seeing the godly family men you have become. Keep putting God first and watch Him do more than you could ever think, ask, or imagine!

To all of my supporters: Much love from me to you for speaking words of encouragement and supporting my calling, purpose, and God-given destiny!

Introduction

Would you like to know the secret to walking in God's favor? There is a powerful weapon we can use to walk in the favor of God and I want to share it with you – a weapon that has given me much peace, joy, excitement, and has literally changed my life!

In 1997 God began to work on my mind and my heart and give me the powerful revelation that HIS voice and presence were tangible every waking moment of my life. Prior to 1997 I had no direction in my life. I was stuck with the mindset that life was supposed to be miserable and that was just the "cards I was dealt". I battled abuse, violence, poverty, and negativity. My outlook on life was "bleak" to say the least. In fact, I really didn't care if I lived or died. I consumed my life with alcohol, drugs, and partying – hoping to somehow escape the pain I was in. But all I created was a miserable life for myself and *I wanted to die*. Ever been there? Beloved, I'm here to tell you that God want us to *live*. Correction, He doesn't just want us to live, He wants us to *thrive*. Just as we need daily bread to live on, we need the powerful weapon of God's Holy Spirit, HIS WORD, the BIBLE, our SWORD! *That* is my secret and *that* is the key to walking in God's favor!

> *And the tempter came and said to Him, "If You are the Son of God, command that these stones become bread." But Jesus replied, "It is written and forever remains written, 'Man shall not live by bread alone, but by every word that comes out of the mouth of God.'"*
>
> - Matthew 4:3-4, (AMP)

> *For the word of God is living and active and full of power [making it operative, energizing, and effective]. It is sharper than any two-edged sword, penetrating as far as the division of the soul and spirit [the **completeness** of*

a person], and of both joints and marrow [the deepest parts of our nature], exposing and judging the very thoughts and intentions of the heart.

- Hebrews 4:12, (AMP)

That's exciting news! Did you catch that? The word of God makes us complete. Through His Word, we are able to combat old negative and wrong mindsets and replace them with a *new* mindset. Thus, leading us to a newness of life! If you are a believer reading this today (or even if you are a non-believer), I encourage you to start reading the Word of God *daily*. I promise you, it will change your life! What do you have to lose?

I wrote this book to share short stories, personal experiences, and what I have learned along the way from my biblical journey. I want to share with you how God uses His Word to change me *daily*. The good news is, He can change you, your world, and your atmosphere too! However, I must be frank with you, the Word of God will not only change you but it will *challenge* you. I say *challenge* because when you are used to a particular thought or mindset, it can be very difficult (and sometimes very painful) to change old habits or thought processes. BUT, when we allow God to do so, it will lead to our *FREEDOM!*

There is no special formula for walking in God's favor, it is simply about reading His Word and applying it to our lives. Through the Bible we learn the character of God, what pleases Him, and what does not. It teaches us what to pursue and what to abstain from in order to have a more victorious life. It reveals to us that there is *great reward* for those who abide in God's Word... that *is* walking in God's favor!

If you walk in My statutes and keep My commandments and [obediently] do them, then I will give you rain in its season, and the land will yield her produce and the trees of the field bear their fruit. And your threshing season will last until grape gathering and the grape gathering [time] will last until planting, and you will eat your bread and be filled and live securely in your land. I will also grant peace in the land, so that you may lie down and there will be no one to make you afraid. I will also eliminate harmful animals from the land, and no sword will pass through your land. And you will chase your enemies, and they will fall before you by the sword.

- Leviticus 26:3-7, (AMP)

But without faith it is impossible to [walk with God and] please Him, for whoever comes [near] to God must [necessarily] believe that God exists and that He rewards those who [earnestly and diligently] seek Him.

- Hebrews 11:6, (AMP)

Are you getting excited yet? Do you feel joy in what God is promising you? In this book, you will notice that I use scripture for every devotional. I encourage you to break out your Bible (and maybe your journal) and read the scriptures for yourself. You may even want to compare different versions (i.e. King James Version vs Amplified vs NIV) and see how it speaks to you. Don't be afraid to underline, highlight, and jot down notes on what God is specifically speaking to you. That is the beauty of walking in God's favor. He desires to speak to you *personally* and give you the blueprint of His plan and purpose for you. He wants you to have a more powerful life!

I hope through these daily devotionals, you can see how God is *eager* to speak to us in our everyday lives. Remember, we are not only to read God's Word, but the way to a more favorable life is to *apply it* to our lives!

But prove yourselves doers of the word [actively and continually obeying God's precepts], and not merely listeners [who hear the word but fail to internalize its meaning], deluding yourselves [by unsound reasoning contrary to the truth]. For if anyone only listens to the word without obeying it, he is like a man who looks very carefully at his natural face in a mirror; for once he has looked at himself and gone away, he immediately forgets what he looked like. But he who looks carefully into the perfect law, the law of liberty, and faithfully abides by it, not having become a [careless] listener who forgets but an active doer [who obeys], he will be blessed and favored by God in what he does [in his life of obedience].

- James 1:22-25, (AMP)

I want to reiterate that the Bible is key for us. As we just read in the above scripture, it is the way to having a blessed and favored life. I sincerely pray that you will not just let this book sit to collect dust, but that you will be diligent in reading your daily devotions. While reading the scriptures, you will see how God's Word is vital to living a strengthened and joyful life. Through sharing my personal testimonies in this daily devotional, you will witness many manifestations of God's working power, protection, and goodness over our lives.

As you read these devotionals (most importantly, along with God's powerful Word), I believe you will begin to hear God's voice, understand His character, and understand His loving plan for your life. May God richly bless you as you move forward in reading His Word and learning the key to walking in God's favor.

HE IS THE GOD THAT SEES YOU

> "Then she called the name of the Lord who spoke to her, 'You are God Who Sees'; for she said, 'Have I not even here [in the wilderness] remained alive after seeing Him [who sees me with understanding and compassion]?'"
> (Genesis 16:13, AMP)

One evening I was getting ready to be a part of a big Christian event in our community. Our committee had specifically planned that we were to wear a *white* t-shirt. Although I hadn't worn it in a while, I knew I had one in the back of my closet somewhere. When it came time to get ready, I perused through my closet and found it. I pulled it over my head, tucked and pulled a little *(okay, ALOT)* until I *finally* got it over my body. But much to my dismay, there was a dilemma. I couldn't move! My arms were stuck straight by my side. I tried to convince myself that the shirt had somehow shrunk while being in my closet. But truth be told, I knew I had acquired a few pounds *(okay okay, maybe more than a few, don't judge)*. The fact is, this just wasn't going to work!

SO, I hurriedly drove to the nearest retail store to hunt down that *white* t-shirt. I have to admit, I was feeling a bit bummed. Thinking about how many sizes I possibly went up made me *cringe*. And to think, *"now I have to get up in front of all these people?!"* I was sure I would be *exposed*. I just knew everyone would know my t-shirt no longer fit. *"How embarrassing!"*, I thought. *"Oh boy, maybe I shouldn't even go to the event at all!"*, I complained *(silly, I know)*. All these negative thoughts kept bombarding my mind as I was browsing through the store.

I finally found the shirt I needed, grabbed it, and quickly stood in line. I was still combatting those negative and accusing thoughts. Well, I shouldn't even say *"combatting"*. I was taking it *all* in. I was believing every single lie... *hook, line, and sinker!*

Finally, I got distracted by something that caught my eye. Next to the cash register was a glass case filled with beautiful jewelry *(God, sure does know how to catch my attention!)*. I admired one particular pair of stud earrings that were in a dazzling aquamarine color. The price tag read, "$50". It was a higher price than I would typically pay for a pair of earrings so I knew I shouldn't get them. I mindlessly just stood there in appreciation of how beautiful they were.

Suddenly, the lady standing behind me in line said, *"I have a coupon if you want to get those."* I stood there looking at her. My mind was still a bit "spaced out". She had to repeat herself so I could grasp what she was saying. Although I appreciated her kind gesture, I knew the earrings would probably still be a bit too high, even with a coupon. Just as I was about to kindly decline her offer, the employee at the register said, *"Let me see that."* She took the coupon from the lady, typed in some numbers on her register, and said, *"That would make the total for those earrings $5!"* I gasped in amazement, *"Wait. Did she say FIVE dollars?"* Now that I could handle! I looked up to the Heavens and smiled. I knew that was *all* God.

This is the point. God sees you. He knows you. Every little thing that concerns you, concerns Him. He knew I was feeling down about my weight. I know it may sound shallow to some, but not to God. He wanted to do a little something for me to make me smile. He wanted to remind me that He *sees* me. It's not just about the jewelry. It's more than that. It's God's reminder that He KNOWS me, SPEAKS to me, and SEES me.

Today I encourage you to expect God to speak to you in the "everyday" things. Even through the little things. He wants to *overwhelm* you. He loves you and He cares for you. He wants to speak to your heart and remind you that He will never leave you nor forsake you (Deuteronomy 31:6). He is the God that sees you!

Lay Down Like the Lion

"God is not man, one given to lies, and not
a son of man changing his mind.
Does he speak and not do what he says? Does
he promise and not come through?
I was brought here to bless; and now he's
blessed—how can I change that?
He has no bone to pick with Jacob, he sees nothing wrong with Israel.
God is with them, and they're with him, shouting praises to their King.
God brought them out of Egypt, rampaging like a wild ox.
No magic spells can bind Jacob, no incantations can hold back Israel.
People will look at Jacob and Israel and say,
"What a great thing has God done!"
Look, a people rising to its feet, stretching like
a lion, a king-of-the-beasts, aroused,
Unsleeping, unresting until its hunt is over
and it's eaten and drunk its fill."
(Numbers 23:17-24, MSG)*

I just love the WORD of GOD. No other book in the World encompasses romance, tragedy, conviction, irony, and humor like the Bible does. Contrary to some beliefs, the Bible is certainly not boring! Reading Numbers 23, you just gotta laugh. Three times Balak wanted the prophet to curse God's people but instead, *three* times all that would come out of the prophet's mouth were blessings, blessings, blessings! Who says God doesn't have a sense of humor?

The *"stretching like a lion"* in this scripture peaked my interest. We often hear of *roaring* like a lion, being as *bold* as a lion, or having the *heart* of a lion, being *courageous* like a lion. But *stretching* like a lion? Huh? So I decided to dig a little further. In my research, this is what I found:

Lions lay down, stretch, and quietly take up residence *wherever* they like. Why? Because they are secure and have no fear of their enemies. They lay down and sleep without any concern of *anything, anywhere,* or *anyone.* But, the lion is no pushover. There is great folly for the one that would dare to stir him up. It would be a very rash, bold, and *dangerous* thing to rouse up a lion lying down.

It is the same with God's people. Because we know *who* we are and *who* we belong to, we should be free of worry, anxiety, and fear. We should not fear our adversaries or those that desire to curse us or cause us harm. We should be able to lay down, rest, and be at peace knowing that God protects us from our enemies. He is, after all, the Lion of all lions. Whoa to those who dare provoke God's people, they will have to deal with the Great Lion!

I hope this encourages you today. Know that you have the King of all by your side. He is more powerful than *anything* or *anyone* in Heaven or on Earth. So go ahead! Be at peace and stretch out, and lay down a while.

The Homeless Man

"The Spirit of the Lord God is upon me, because the Lord has anointed *and* qualified me to preach the Gospel *of* good tidings to the meek, the poor, *and* afflicted; He has sent me to bind up *and* heal the brokenhearted, to proclaim liberty to the [physical and spiritual] captives and the opening of the prison *and* of the eyes to those who are bound, to proclaim the acceptable year of the Lord [the year of His favor] and the day of vengeance of our God, to comfort all who mourn..."
(Isaiah 61:1-2, AMP)

Although I have read this scripture over and over again, held it near and dear to my heart, and even recited it a few times; never has it been made so personal to me as when I came face to face with a homeless man.

God must have been preparing me because I recalled having a particular dream. In this dream, God's people were rushing in and out of a (church) building that had a revolving door. People were rushing in and out, in and out of this revolving door. I mean, God's people were really *really* busy! However right outside the door, was a homeless man that no one seemed to take notice of (stay with me here). It seemed as if everyone was on a tight schedule and were simply too focused on the task at hand. I stood watching in amazement. Just then, I heard the Lord's voice beckoning me to sit with the homeless man adding, "and stay a while". So I did. No one else really seemed to notice (or care - for that matter). Soon after, I awoke from my dream and just tucked it away in my heart.

A few weeks later I was invited to attend a Christian conference. We stayed at this beautiful hotel (which was packed full with other believers that were also attending this conference). We had a tight schedule so our first evening there, we hurriedly got ready and out the *revolving door* we went. As soon as I stepped outside, there he was! To my astonishment, it was the homeless man from my dream! I *knew* I was supposed to visit with him but couldn't build up the nerve... I mean after all, there were *all* these people around coming in and out, in and out of that revolving door. We were all just trying to keep in line with that *jam packed* conference schedule.

Honestly, it just didn't seem like a convenient time. So to my own disappointment, I simply passed him up (being careful to make *no* eye contact in the process). But yet, my heart was grieved. I prayed to God and asked Him to please forgive me and to *please* give me a second chance. *This* time I will stop and talk to him, *I promise*.

So the next day, to my amazement, there the homeless man was *again*! I tried to build up the nerve (I mean, I really *really* tried) but once again, I simply passed him up (once again being careful to make *no* eye contact). And once again, I begged the Lord to give me just *one... more... chance*. *This* time I will be obedient!

So as gracious as God is, wouldn't you know it that the *next* day (and for the *third* time), God would allow me to run into the homeless man, *again*. I took a deep breath and braced myself. I stopped right in front of him and begin to offer him food or coffee, but he wanted none of it. I awkwardly struck up a conversation and we began chatting a bit. At one point, his cold hard frown began to turn into an upward grin, maybe even a smile. He didn't seem to want anything monetarily from me.

Truth be told, my "super-spiritual" self wanted to "beat him over the head" with bible versus and scripture, but I didn't. I didn't feel the Holy Spirit leading me to and I felt strongly I was to obey. Although I did share that I belonged to Jesus and God had put him on my heart, I felt I was to simply listen more than I was to speak (or *preach*). As I listened intently, I observed that small glimmer of hope in his eye. I couldn't help but notice the deeply imbedded scars and wrinkles on his face. He wasn't an old man per se, just a man that had obviously been through much turmoil, tragedy, and despair. Years of having a *hard life* now revealed itself on his face (physically and emotionally).

As we finished our conversation and I walked away, I asked the Lord what the point of it all was. He reminded me of a book I read long ago where a homeless man began to believe he was invisible. He said in essence, *"no one seemed to take notice, no one seemed to care"*.

The Lord began to show me that every wrinkle and scar on that homeless man's face (by this time, a new friend by the name of "Clark") represented God's broken people. He said, "Never again will you walk by my broken people without taking notice." I was *undone. Broken. Overwhelmed.* I wept... wept uncontrollably. Gut-wrenched with the idea of hurriedly passing by many *many* hurting and broken people that I didn't "take notice" of. I share my story because I want to implore you to no longer just pass by the poor, the broken-hearted, the prostitute, the homeless. The world is waiting for us to take notice through God's eyes. Today I encourage you to *see* who the Lord is sending *you* to!

"No one has ever seen me before. God has sent you to see me."

BONDAGE BREAKER

"He forgives your sins - Every. Single. One."
(Psalm 103:5)

Isn't it amazing, that God, the Judge of Good and Evil is quick to forgive? Your spouse may not want to forgive you. That co-worker may still be mad at you. Your friend may not want to talk to you or forgive you... but GOD, *He* is quick to forgive... every single sin. He won't hold it against you. Once we ask for forgiveness, it's done, never to be brought to us again.

The thought is humbling. There are people who may have done us wrong... *big time*. We may at times wish for the "offender" to get what they deserve. We cry out to God to pour out His wrath and bring them to justice.

But then we remember, *our* sin, *our* offenses and how quick God was to forgive the "unforgivable" in *us*. Who then, are *we* that we would not forgive others when the Almighty has forgiven *us*? To truly love and forgive is to know the One that has loved and forgiven us.

When we choose the path of unforgiveness, we cling on to bitterness, hate, and resentment. This doesn't affect the "offender". It affects *us*. Unforgiveness keeps our heart bound in the shackles of distrust, insecurities, and fear. We then begin to have a distorted outlook in how we view others, how we view ourselves, and most importantly - how we view God.

Jesus said to forgive seventy times seven because no matter how much you forgive others, he has forgiven you even more (Matthew 18:12).

Today I encourage you to seek your heart and allow God to show you areas where you may be holding on to unforgiveness. Ask Him to take it from you and to heal you. Do not be held in bondage *any longer.* Jesus wants to heal your heart that you may *BE. SET. FREE.* Forgive others just as He has forgiven you and allow Jesus to break the chains of unforgiveness. He is, after all, the Bondage Breaker!

What Can I Expect from God?

"I have made a covenant with my eyes; Why then should I look upon a young woman? For what is the allotment of God from above, And the inheritance of the Almighty from on high? Is it not destruction for the wicked, And disaster for the workers of iniquity? Does He not see my ways, And count all my steps? If I have despised the cause of my male or female servant when they complained against me, what then shall I do when God rises up? When He punishes, how shall I answer Him? Did not He who made me in the womb make them? Did not the same One fashion us in the womb? The fear of God has kept me from these things - how else could I ever face Him?"
(Job 31:1-4, 13-15, 23, NKJV)

Job begins this scripture with proclaiming his innocence from sins of the heart, lusts, perversions, or from cheating in business or in marriage. He understood the spiritual nature of God's commandments. He reveals genuine concern for those in need and recognizes that power and influence must not be abused but used to help the less fortunate.

So what was the reason for his plight? Although he was accused by his friends, Job was not guilty of any hypocrisy or violence. He declared his uprightness and his integrity. He was not boastful, but instead, was bold in answering his accusers.

Job courageously speaks of what is good and his sincerity in it. He understood that when people gain dishonestly; they will sow wheat, but reap thistles. He boldly refutes the accusations against his moral and religious character as the cause for his sufferings.

Although there is a principle of "sowing and reaping", illness and tragedy strikes because we live in a sinful and broken world that was cursed long ago back in Genesis. As we can see through the example of Job, suffering is not always a direct reflection of sin.

Well meaning believers often accuse others of somehow "being out of God's will" when illness or tragedy strikes. However, no matter their confidence during their accusations, they are sadly mistaken. Personally, I've been appalled at some of the things Christians will say to the already downtrodden and broken-hearted...."*You must be out of God's will!*", they accuse. "*You must have unforgiveness in your heart!*", they shout. "*You must be in sin!*", they proclaim. If you have experienced this, I am deeply sorry for your heart ache. This type of mindset comes from an arrogant and prideful heart (for anyone to conclude their righteousness is the reason tragedy hasn't struck them is atrocious). Let's be honest, if sin alone is the reason for suffering, shouldn't we all be walking around with illness and tragedy? Which one of us is truly without sin? How well do you keep the Ten Commandments?

So what can we expect from God? We can expect HIS salvation from our sin and from ourselves. We can expect HIS justice and faithfulness. We can expect HIS presence and HIS compassion toward us. We can expect HIS love and that HE has our best interest at heart.

You Are Loved

> "The LORD your God is in your midst, a mighty one who will save; he will rejoice over you with gladness; he will quiet you by his love; he will exult over you with loud singing."
> (Zephaniah 3:17)

One afternoon as I was out running some errands, I saw a woman with a beautiful short silver necklace around her neck. It was a plain dainty necklace that simply read, "love". It caught my attention as I thought it was a beautiful necklace, even in its simplicity but I really didn't think much more about it.

A few days later, I had one of my (dreaded) doctor's appointment. During this time in my life, I was going through a lot of health issues (and questioning God) and quite frankly I was feeling a bit "blah".

After my appointment, I stopped at a retail store to get a few household items. I was an hour away from home so I hurriedly rushed in to get what I needed. However, as I walked down one of the aisles, I caught a little "glimmer" in my peripheral vision. I really wasn't paying much attention but as I turned to look, I saw a table with a few items for sale. Then I saw *the* necklace I had seen earlier in the week in *my favorite* metal! The only (BIG) difference is that it read "loveD" instead of "love". Oh, I really loved it but reluctantly decided I needed to "stay on track" and forget about the beautiful necklace.

However, as I passed the table, I *clearly* heard the Lord say, "I want you to have it. It is my gift to you. A reminder to you that you are loveD by your FATHER". I knew what He meant (especially considering I had little relationship with my own earthly father). It was such a sweet and precious moment for me. My eyes welled up as I fought back the tears. I felt so special to Him. There were several other *similar* "love" necklaces but I knew this one was especially for me. It was the only one that was in my favorite metal, and the only one that read "loveD" (meaning *already* loveD).

God speaks to us in many ways. It doesn't have to be through a necklace... it could be through a beautiful flower you find on your daily walk. It could be through a trusted & loyal friend. It could be through a good movie with a heart felt message. We can have many material things in this world, but when we don't have a relationship with God or know His love for us, then it's all as of nothing. When we don't know true and real love from the FATHER, we lack authenticity, we are critical, judgmental, envious, and mean towards others. When we truly know who we are, when we know the love of the Father, when we know that we are already loveD by HIM; we know how to effectively love others with genuine compassion, understanding, free of judgement, free of criticism, and with a heart of forgiveness.

Just wanted to share a little bit of God's goodness with you today and to remind you that you ARE loveD.

The .05 Cent Bubble Gum

"Remember that the Lord will reward each one of us for
the good we do, whether we are slaves or free."
(Ephesians 6:8, NLT)

When I was a little girl, I would often ride my bike to the corner gas station. Sometimes mom would send me there on an errand. Other times, I would just stop in to buy myself some pop (or a "coke" - as us Texans often say it).

Now, I typically would have to save up my pennies to buy myself something, so to have enough money for that bubbly black stuff was a real treat. I must admit, my mouth often salivated as I went up and down that candy aisle but I knew I only had enough money for *one thing*.

One particular afternoon, on my frequent visit to the gas station, the owner said to me, "You can have whatever you want in the store. Pick something. *Whatever* you want." I was astonished. "Did he mean *for free? Is this some sort of trick?*", I thought. I was bashful. I didn't want to take anything. But he insisted. For the life of me, I couldn't fathom such a kind gesture from the "funny accented" man - so I asked him *why*. He responded, "I see a lot of kids from the neighborhood come in and out of here and they always try to steal from me". He said, "I have kept my eye on you and not once have you ever tried stealing from me."

My heart bubbled over. Quite honestly, I felt humbled. I didn't want to take anything. I was just doing the right thing. But I settled on the cheapest thing in the store... a piece of .05 cent bubble gum. I'm pretty sure I rode my bike with a smile on my face the whole way home.

Even now, I get choked up thinking about it. You see, it really wasn't about the bubble gum. It was the fact that the store owner took notice. I was by no means a perfect child, but I did do a lot of things *right*. Yet, I thought no one ever seemed to take notice. Still, I always feared doing the wrong thing, even when I thought no one was watching. Maybe it was the fear of God (or the fear of mom), but either way, it didn't feel good to do the wrong thing.

As Christians, we ought to do the right thing, even when we think no one is watching. Truth be told, someone is *always* watching. The world watches to see if this "Jesus thing" is real. People stop to watch and see if Christians are real. As God's people, we are to always choose to do the right thing, no matter how difficult or painful it can be. We shouldn't do it to get recognition from man, but with sincerity of heart in obedience to Christ. After-all, we know we serve God, not men and the reward He carries with Him is a great one for those that choose to do good.

Maybe you are feeling discouraged today. Maybe you feel like you are always doing good and no one seems to take notice. Maybe you think satisfying the flesh is "no big deal". I'm here to tell you, GOD notices. Don't steal a worthless item in exchange for God's great and *valuable* reward. It's not worth it. His reward is always greater. Just be patient. Give it some time. Your reward is coming!

Life is Beautiful

> "He has made everything beautiful in its time. He has also set eternity in the human heart; yet no one can fathom what God has done from beginning to end." (Ecclesiastes 3:11, NIV)

> "Therefore I tell you, do not worry about your life, what you will eat or drink; or about your body, what you will wear. Is not life more than food, and the body more than clothes? Look at the birds of the air; they do not sow or reap or store away in barns, and yet your heavenly Father feeds them. Are you not much more valuable than they? (Matt 6:25-26, NIV)

God has made "everything beautiful in its time". Did you catch that? *Everything*.

It is difficult to conceive how everything can be made beautiful when we are living in a world of poverty, loss, heartbreak, violence, sickness and disease. Even Christians often struggle with the age old question of, *"How can a good God allow such bad things to happen in life?"*

Catastrophic events or the tragedies we experience in life does not negate the fact that God is still good. Even in the midst of tragedy, God *still* has a beautiful plan for our lives. In fact, sometimes the beauty of life is not revealed until we see God take the broken pieces of our broken hearts and create something beautiful out of it... something that only He can do.

He takes a withered tree and allows it to bloom again. He takes a broken body and allows it to heal again. He takes a broken home and restores it again. He takes disappointment and gives hope again. He takes the defiled and makes it clean again. Yes, in the midst of it all, "Life is *still* beautiful" because we serve a beautiful God that will turn *all* things for our good in due season.

No matter what you are going through, know that God will not limit you. He will not limit the plans He has for your life because He deeply loves you and cares about you. He will heal the memories filled with pain. As human beings, we can only see a small part of God's greater work. Recognizing our limitations enables us to trust God and His work. All the while, even with great uncertainty, let us have faith and trust in God with the ability to say, "Yes, Life is *still* beautiful".

The Cleft of the Rock

"But you may not see the glory of my face, for man may not see me and live. However, stand here on this rock beside me. And when my glory goes by, I will put you in the cleft of the rock and cover you with my hand until I have passed. Then I will remove my hand, and you shall see my back but not my face." (Exodus 33:20-23, TLB)

God's response to Moses is one filled with compassion and grace. God is actually granting Moses' bold request to the furthest extent that mankind can handle it.

Of all my travels, one of my favorite pictures is one where I am standing under the cleft of the rock at the Grand Canyon. As I was making my way down the canyon, I came across a cleft that allowed me to take a rest, sip my water, and cool down. It was a nice breather from the harsh heat of the desert sun.

As I leaned into the rock, I noticed the rugged surfaces that had constantly been exposed to the fury and heat of the day. Yet inside the cleft, it was cool and the rock was smooth in comparison - untouched and protected.

I have often heard of the scripture in Exodus but not so sure I fully understood the meaning of being, "in the cleft of the rock". Until that moment, I never really thought about what it meant to be hiding in the cleft. However, in an instant, I had a heart connection with the scripture I had so often previously read. I realized that if the storm beat around me or if the harshness of life seemed too unbearable, I wanted to be in the cleft of the rock... and covered by God's almighty hand.

We cannot see God in the midst of our storm, but yet, He is there protecting us from things we are not aware of. Often times it is not until we are out of our precarious situation that we see God pass by and are left marveling at His awesome works and presence. At that moment, we are left smiling, looking up to the heavens and saying, "Yeah, that was you God".

If you are going through a perilous situation in your life today, do not fear. God covers you with His Almighty hand and places you in the cleft of the rock. You may not see it for a little while, but while you are there, rest and trust.

Keeping Up With Appearances

> "But the Lord told Samuel, 'Don't look at his appearance or how tall he is, because I have rejected him. God does not see as humans see. Humans look at outward appearances, but the Lord looks into the heart.'" (1 Samuel 16:7, GW)

Can you imagine discovering that your family has had a dinner without you because you were considered the "runt" of the family? (1 Sam 16:11, MSG). This was the case with David and the term his father used to describe him. Can you imagine how painful it would be to hear those words and experience that type of rejection from your own family members?

David had the responsibility of tending to his father's sheep so he didn't always appear as "clean-cut" as his father had hoped. It was evident that his father took some pride in the way his "better-looking" brothers carried themselves. David was often looked down upon and considered to be "less than".

Shepherds had dirty jobs. There wasn't much water in the desert, so bathing would be considered a luxury. Sheep's wool is often dirty and oily, so it would be difficult for a shepherd to remain clean. The fact that they couldn't bath properly and were constantly dealing with blood and the birthing of baby sheep kept them ritually unclean (what an image)! The Jewish law required seven days away from blood in order to enter the temple and worship God. So as you can imagine, shepherds didn't fit the "church-goer" mold. They were, in many respects, despised by the general public, even while providing an essential service for society. They were always dirty and considered to be lower class citizens.

Interestingly enough, the one that wasn't "fit" to attend the dinner party is the one God used to lead the nation of Israel into spiritual and political victory. David was well respected and became famous in all of Israel.

Among all the brothers, God chose David to become king, the less likely of them all (God is in the business of doing that)!

Even Jesus, "had no beauty or majesty to attract us to him, nothing in his appearance that we should desire him" (Isaiah 53:2, NIV) but God used our Shepherd to become dirty so that He may lay down His life for us "dirty" sheep.

Too often believers are overly concerned with how things appear on the *outside* as a means to try to impress others. Pride tells us that we have to pretend to be *perfect* while dealing with family, church, work, or friends. We want everyone to think we have it *all* together. Beloved, that is an exhausting way to live! It is a facade that many can see through and it really doesn't impress anyone anyway. Don't wear yourself out trying to "keep up appearances".

What we *should* be overly concerned with is allowing the Lord to search our heart and reveal the things that are disingenuous. Unfortunately, man's flesh always wants to judge according to appearances, but he Lord is concerned with our character and the inner thoughts of our heart.

Today I encourage you to get out of your comfort zone and formulate a conversation with someone you wouldn't typically converse with. You may be surprised how God can use the "less likely" in your life to bring about victory, freedom, and salvation. After all, the less likely is someone like King David. Most importantly, the less likely is someone like King Jesus. And maybe, just maybe, the "less likely" is someone like you!

God's Grace

"Therefore no one will be declared righteous in his sight by observing the law; rather, through the law we become conscious of sin. But now a righteousness from God, apart from law, has been made known, to which the Law and the Prophets testify. This righteousness from God comes through faith in Jesus Christ to all who believe. There is no difference, for all have sinned and fall short of the glory of God, and are justified freely by his grace through the redemption that came by Christ Jesus." (Romans 3:20-24, NIV)

On particular afternoon, I was driving down the highway when one of my favorite songs came on the radio. It was a pretty upbeat song so I mindlessly began a shaken and a moving. Well, I guess I must've been tapping the gas pedal a little too heavily because before I knew it, I see those flashing red and blue lights in my rear view mirror. "Surely", I thought, "this cop got an emergency call and *that* is the reason for the bright lights". So I move over to the next lane *and* he follows me.

Apparently, I was going over the speed limit (*way* over the speed limit - more than I would like to admit over the speed limit). My vehicle didn't have its tags yet and my license was from another State. I could see how the timing of it all looked suspicious but they were all innocent scenarios (*really!*) But nonetheless, I knew I was *done*. I was a nervous wreck. In fact, I was so nervous that when the police officer asked me for my license, I accidentally handed him my credit card (bribery, anyone?)! But I must say, he was probably the nicest cop who has ever pulled me over. I obviously didn't *want* a speeding ticket but his kindness helped calm my nerves a bit.

I waited in my car for what seems like *hours*. The officer returns only to hand me a *warning* slip and tells me to "have a good day". *"Have a good day? NO ticket?!!"* I was dumbfounded.

As I drove away, God began speaking to me about His grace. You see, His grace gives us *way* more than we deserve. I *deserved* a ticket. But what I received was a "free pass". Now, does that mean after the police officer left I kept speeding? You bet not! I was so grateful. This time, I made sure I was paying attention, being more aware. It's the same with God. Because of breaking HIS laws and being in sin, we deserve hell. But because of Jesus, we can have Heaven! That is part of God's eternal grace. He gives us *more* than we deserve. However, is that a "free pass" to keep doing wrong in sin? Absolutely not! When we truly understand God's grace and what He has done for us on the cross, we don't *want* to sin. We are so grateful for undeserved grace that we don't want to sin again, we want to be more aware of Him. When we truly understand His love, mercy, forgiveness, and grace, we are left dumbfounded.

Drowning in His Presence

> "I will use my power against Judah and against those who live in Jerusalem. I will remove the faithful few of Baal from this place and the names of the pagan priests along with my priests. I will remove those who worship all the stars in the sky on their rooftops and those who worship by swearing loyalty to the Lord while also swearing loyalty to the god Milcom. I will remove those who have turned away from following the Lord and those who no longer seek the Lord or ask him for help."
> (Zephaniah 1:4-6, GW)

As humans, we often search for *someone* or *something* that will give us hope, inspiration, encouragement, and the blueprint for the next step of our lives. We want to find that *thing* that will give us an edge in the dog-eat-dog competitive world we live in. There are many resources that have been promoted and marketed with both zeal and skill that teaches us how we can keep our "business" and our "lives" booming.

However, as believers, these are the very things that God often wants to "root out" of our lives. Because the *root* of every Christian's life should be a solid spiritual life that is embedded in a relationship with Christ. Everything we do, think, or feel has to do with God. Every *person* we meet has to do with God.

We are surrounded by and are *drowning* in His presence, yet we fail to see it. There are too many distractions and too many noises that often hinders us from experiencing Him. Turn off the television, the radio, and the video games. We may not intentionally worship the god Milcom, but these distractions often do become idols of worship. Don't worry about connecting to the internet, connect with the Almighty. I wonder how many of us are so desperate for a glimpse of His presence that we would be willing to throw away the "to do" list, take a different route, plan a different day, throw away our preconceived agendas for ourselves and for our children and abide in His perfect will and presence. I wonder what it would look like if we threw our goals out the window, surrendered our arms to the sky and said, "Lord, just do whatever will bring you the most glory".

I realize shutting out the noise of the world takes work. However, it is time that believers put a "do not disturb" sign on the doorposts of our spirits, seek the Lord, ask Him for help, and put a stop to everything that hinders us from drowning in His presence.

COMPARISON, THE THIEF OF CONTENTMENT

"For we dare not class ourselves or compare ourselves with those who commend themselves. But they, measuring themselves by themselves, and comparing themselves among themselves, are not wise."
(2 Corinthians 10:12, NKJV)

Paul warned the church of Corinth against comparing themselves to one another as it is "not wise". Comparison robs a person from joy and contentment in their lives. It can lead to greedy pursuits, make a person vulnerable to temptation, and can cause a person great grief. The car they once appreciated, is no longer good enough when a family member gets a newer model. The house they were so content with is no longer "cutting it" when the neighbor does a remodel. Or that healthy body is loathed when a co-worker starts noticeably losing weight. Or the church attendance of 100 people is no longer as exciting as the church with 500 people down the road. The list can go on and on.

Paul said it well in Philippians 4:11-12, *"Not that I was ever in need, for I have learned how to get along happily whether I have much or little. I know how to live on almost nothing or with everything. I have learned the secret of contentment in every situation, whether it be a full stomach or hunger, plenty or want..."*

Paul modeled a great example of how Christians should act in their relationship with Christ and with one another. Christians should be confident with God's provision and expect contentment in their lives. This godly contentment does not eradicate an ambitious pursuit of God's will in life. But encourage believers to walk so closely with the Lord that we can be content with anything, to live above things, and to be unaffected by circumstance.

Most often, when an individual struggles with a spirit of comparison, it stems from having low self-esteem. The individual views themselves poorly (bad, condemning feelings about themselves). These are "weights" that keep a believer under condemnation and causes them to be less than God intended.

A believer who has a healthy self-esteem makes no room for comparison. They are confident in knowing (and accepting) that God has created each individual with unique strengths and weaknesses. They can appreciate the differences in others and do not let a spirit of comparison ruin good relationships.

God does not evaluate human life and worth as we do. Our society is caught up in a whirlwind of titles, prestige, and salaries. An individual with good self-esteem is content with whatever God has in their life. Instead of breaking out the measuring sticks and comparing ourselves with one another, believers should celebrate each other and help one another reach their maximum potential.

Fingerprints of God

✠

"Do not hide Your face from me, Do not turn Your servant away in anger; You have been my help; Do not abandon me nor forsake me, O God of my salvation! For my father and my mother have forsaken me, But the LORD will take me up. (Psalm 27:9-10, NASB)

Let me great real and personal here for a moment. Not too long ago, I was at a place in my life where I was having difficulty seeing, hearing, and *feeling* God's presence. I was combatting many battles. I felt isolated and alone. I was encountering one set back after another and I just couldn't seem to catch a break *(ever been there?)*.

Finally, after several months, things started to *somewhat* get back to normal. I started to hear God's voice again. I started to feel His presence again. I was so delighted. My heart flipped with joy. But I was confused as to why I didn't experience Him during the times I felt I needed Him the most. So I simply asked Him, "God, where have you been? Why haven't I felt your presence?"

He said simply, "Your despair had overshadowed my presence". It took me a minute to understand. But once I got it, I was dumbfounded. It made perfect sense!

You see, our feelings are fickle. We are up one day and down the next. Sometimes we are on the mountaintop and sometimes we are in the valley. It's not that *He* wasn't present, it's just that I wasn't able to *feel* His presence because of all the turmoil and distractions in my life. *That* is what I was feeling and seeing and *focusing* on.

True faith knows God is present (even during times we cannot see or feel Him).

No matter what you are going through, I want to encourage you today. God *is* present! Don't let whatever is trying to take you down overshadow God's presence and LOVE for you! You may not see *where* God is or *what* He is doing, but beloved, know that He is there. He hasn't left you or forsaken you. Know that God is working in the midst and has His fingerprints *all over you*!

Wrestling in the Spirit

"Finally, receive your power from the Lord and from his mighty strength. Put on all the armor that God supplies. In this way you can take a stand against the devil's strategies. This is not a wrestling match against a human opponent. We are wrestling with rulers, authorities, the powers who govern this world of darkness, and spiritual forces that control evil in the heavenly world. For this reason, take up all the armor that God supplies. Then you will be able to take a stand during these evil days. Once you have overcome all obstacles, you will be able to stand your ground." (Ephesians 6:10-13, GW)

Too often, we as believers try to fight off spiritual obstacles by natural means. This will never work. The end result is tirelessly fighting a battle that is never ending. Human effort is inadequate but God's invincible power is more real than anything that is seen.

Ever feel like you can't catch a break? Car breaks down, kids are sick, bad performance at work, someone is mad at you.... and that's just all in one day. The combat is not against human enemies, but against satan's assaults. Satan knows the good things God has for your future and the enemy spends his days seeking to and fro someone he can lure into temptation, bring discouragement, and get off of God's track. Beloved, don't let that be you.

Christians must be armed for defense in battle *daily*. So what are our weapons of attack?

First and foremost, we have the sword of the Spirit, which is the word of God. The word of God divides the truth from the lies of the enemy. It gives us the tools in how to fight against the spiritual warfare we encounter daily. You and I have an enemy that is going to do everything in his power to prevent us from living the way God wants us to live. Satan wants to thwart the purposes of God in our lives. He hates God and manifest that hate in attempting to thwart the purposes of God that are basically operational in us. And so his assault against us is primarily an assault against God. We need the word of God to give us insight of the enemies schemes and how to come against them.

Our second weapon of attack is *prayer*. When we pray, we command the heavenlies. Angels stand at attention waiting for our every command and begin to battle on our behalf. Prayer is powerful and can move mountains! Prayer is direct communication with God. The power of prayer is the constant renewal of perspective. Prayer opens our eyes. It extends our horizons. It sheds light into the darkness of our fears and our sorrows, our hopes and joys, our shame and our pride. It gives us new ways of seeing life, relationships, and divine insight into understanding spiritual warfare.

Our third weapon of attack is the Holy Spirit. God promises to give us guidance and wise counsel through His Holy Spirit. It is important to listen to the silent alarms that go off within us that say, "don't go there", "don't do that", "don't align yourself with that individual". No matter how small the situation may appear, it can be the cause of *great* consequence when it comes to spiritual warfare.

LIGHT IN A DARK WORLD

"You are light for the world. A city cannot be hidden when it is located on a hill. No one lights a lamp and puts it under a basket. Instead, everyone who lights a lamp puts it on a lamp stand. Then its light shines on everyone in the house. In the same way let your light shine in front of people. Then they will see the good that you do and praise your Father in heaven."
(Matthew 5:14-16, GW)

Quite often believers are taught, "Only associate in Christian circles", "Do not go out into the world", "Let's shine our light on one another". This is *so* contrary to the word of God and extremely ineffective. We must be the light in the midst of a dark world. Shining our light on one another is of no benefit as we know that the light shines brightest in the midst of darkness. It's time for Christians to stop hiding from the very world that Jesus sent us to go into.

The world is *dying* for a people that will have the answer in the midst of broken humanity. Don't like politics? YOU are the answer. To much crime? YOU are the answer. Disappointed in our education system? YOU are the answer. Too much propaganda? YOU are the answer. Christians all over the world are waiting for the world to change. Yet, the world is so desperately waiting for Christians to shine their light brightly and change the world. Instead, we remain "hidden" in our homes, in our churches, and in the marketplace.

Many of us are looking for miracles and revival when we fail to practice basic Christianity. The motto is often, "Lord, do your thing as I sit here and do absolutely nothing." God never called darkness to change the world. He called us as believers to be the light of the world, changing the atmosphere around us. It's OUR job to change the world.

As Christians, sometimes God redirects our steps according to His will and plans. It can be disheartening to see fear creep into the body of Christ and hear comments like, "Well, we've never done it that way before..." If that's the case, than *good*! Doing things differently than they've always been done gives God the opportunity to do a new thing and utilize us in a different way to impact the world. Allowing words of doubt and unbelief to crawl into our church body destroys our God given destiny more than anything else. So don't hide that light of yours, let it shine, shine, shine!

A Treacherous Heart

"Adonijah, the son of Haggith, came to Bathsheba, the mother of Solomon. She said, 'Do you come peaceably?' And he said, 'Peaceably'. He said, 'I have something to say to you'. And she said, 'Say on'. He said, 'You know that the kingdom belonged to me [as the eldest living son], and all Israel looked to me to reign. However, the kingdom has passed from me to my brother; for it was his from the Lord. Now I make one request of you; do not deny me'. And she said, 'Say on'. He said, 'I pray you, ask King Solomon, for he will not refuse you, to give me Abishag the Shunammite to be my wife'... Then King Solomon swore by the Lord, saying, 'May God do so to me, and more also, if Adonijah has not requested this against his own life. Therefore, as the Lord lives, Who has established me and set me on the throne of David my father and Who has made me a house as He promised, Adonijah shall be put to death this day.'"
(2 Kings 13-17, 23-24, AMP)

Appointing Adonijah to death for his request seemed like such a harsh sentence given by Solomon. After all, it was customary for the older brother to receive the kingdom and Adonijah was willing to let the kingdom go.... or was he?

Actually, Adonijah's request was treacherous and demonstrates that Abishag was legally David's concubine. Notice how Adonijah began his conversation with Bathsheba saying, "You know that the kingdom belonged to *me*... Israel looked to *me* to reign." His motives were self-centered and it was obvious that he felt that something that belonged to him was taken from him. However interestingly, he acknowledges that it was the *Lord* that had given Solomon the kingdom. Yet still, he was conveying the message of, "You owe me something". His request was a scheme in an attempt to gain the throne (which he had tried previously before). It was evident that he set his *own* self up as king. He was king in his *own* eyes. Beloved, any time we place ourselves in a higher position than we ought (whether physically or mentally), we are setting ourselves up for danger... especially if we have not yet been appointed by the Lord.

Solomon pronounced Adonijah to death because he could see his heart in the matter. Adonijah had several opportunities to show himself a worthy man... yet he still believed the throne belonged to him. Chances are that Adonijah would be a constant adversary and a threat to the kingdom since he felt he had been "robbed" and was greatly embittered.

In the same instance, believers should be careful in not becoming territorial when it comes to certain areas that the Lord has entrusted to others (albeit at church, home, with family, or in the workplace). God himself has given that individual(s) authority over that domain, irregardless of tradition or what has always been done in the past. When Christians hold on to bitterness, unforgiveness, don't want to let go, or act upon self-centered fears, the result is a certain spiritual death and that individual cannot move forward to the next "kingdom" the Lord wants to entrust to them.

Today I encourage you to pray about the areas in your life that you need to let go of. Pray with a heart of purity that God will place the right people in their rightful positions, even if that means having to let go.

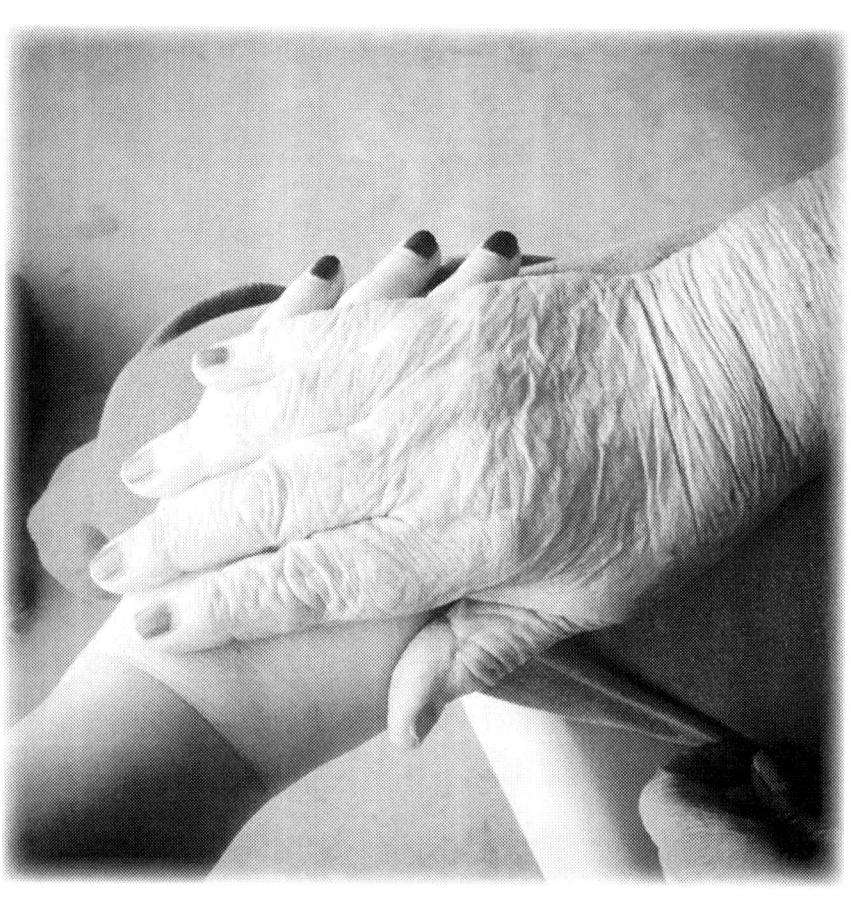

These Hands
(A Tribute to My Grandmother)

"The proverbs (truths obscurely expressed, maxims)
of Solomon son of David, king of Israel:
To know [skillful and godly] wisdom and instruction;
To discern *and* comprehend the words of understanding *and* insight,
To receive instruction in wise behavior *and* the
discipline of wise thoughtfulness,
Righteousness, justice, and integrity;
That prudence (good judgment, astute common sense) may be
given to the naive *or* inexperienced [who are easily misled],
And knowledge and discretion (intelligent discernment) to the youth,
The wise will hear and increase their learning,
And the person of understanding will acquire wise counsel *and*
the skill [to steer his course wisely and lead others to the truth],
To understand a proverb and a figure [of speech]
or an enigma with its interpretation,
And the words of the wise and their riddles [that require reflection].
The [reverent] fear of the Lord [that is, worshiping Him and
regarding Him as truly awesome] is the beginning *and* the
preeminent part of knowledge [its starting point and its essence];
But arrogant [a]fools despise [skillful and godly]
wisdom and instruction *and* self-discipline.
(Proverbs 1:1-7, AMP)

These hands. These hands helped her momma cook in the kitchen and help sew her sisters' dresses (made out of flour sacks) when she was a young girl. These hands held her siblings hands and played on railroad tracks where great-grandpa worked. These hands often braided her sisters' hair and twirled beautiful colorful ribbons around them.

Later in life, these hands were given in marriage and then nursed, bathed, and fed 7 little ones (yes, *SEVEN!*). These hands cleaned house, ironed and folded laundry, and changed several "poopie" diapers.

Eventually she was left with just her and her seven littles so these hands worked *two* jobs tirelessly just to make ends meet. Somehow, these hands still found time to wipe away many little tears (many times, her own).

As her kids grew older and started having families of their own, these hands hugged and squeezed (and sometimes *spanked*) her precious grandchildren (all thirteen of them, yes, *thirteen*)! These hands made big "gourmet" meals out of "whatever is left in the refrigerator", fed her family and her neighbors too *(no joke!)*. These hands embraced all who entered her home, no matter their race, social status, or background (just don't cross her)!

I have gained much wisdom through my grandmother. I have learned to love God, to give to others, to be kind, to be strong, to cook, to love, to be responsible, to be honest, to work hard, and much *much* more. Her feistiness? Well, I learned that one from grandma too!

Now grandma's getting older. She finally got that home she's always wanted (bought for her by one of her grandchildren). But don't think she has slowed down any... oh no. She is the matriarch of the family (in her quiet gentle way). Her children and grandchildren are always calling to check in on her or dropping by to see how she is doing. She is taken shopping, out to eat, to get her hair and nails done, and whatever else she wants. Some (jokingly) say grandma is spoiled, but I don't think so. I think she is just now reaping the love she has always sowed into others.

I just love hearing grandma's stories and the wisdom they entail. It doesn't matter how old we get, we still need the older and wiser gray-haired people in our lives. We should cherish every little moment for we do not know how much time we have with them.

Today I encourage you to take some time for the older people in your life. Don't count them out. God still has them here for a reason. Those years of life experience and the wisdom that comes with it isn't easily obtained. It would be wise to glean some wisdom while you can. And who knows, you may even enjoy their company and have more in common than you think.

Who Shall You Follow?

*"Pattern yourselves after me [follow my example], as
I imitate and follow Christ (the Messiah)."*
(1 Corinthians 11:1, AMP)

Speaking to the church of Corinth, Paul described that his mission was simply to follow after Christ, proving to us all that we can live authentic Christian lives in this world.

Paul addressed problems in the church of Corinth as believers had experienced a church that was torn apart by factions and spiritual immaturity. Prior to receiving the gospel, the Corinthians had a reputation for being unruly promiscuous drunkards... and they brought their mess right back into the church.

When people become Christians, they don't instantaneously become "nice" (this may come as a shock to some people). We must carefully consider that we are all a work in progress... until the day we take our last breath. Conversion to Christ doesn't automatically make people holy. God designed it that way so we may daily see our need for Him and have a continual relationship with Him.

Many of us struggle with living each day as authentic followers of Christ. We are living in a dying world where a generation is *yearning* to discover a group of people who are living a life of authenticity. Shouldn't that be God's people? God wants to work on us from the inside out (not from the outside in - smiling on the outside but gritting our teeth on the inside). Most people can see past the facade. Let's be real. *Trying* to live a Christian life can be exhausting. *Truly* living a Christian life (shortcomings and all) can be liberating. Too often Christians wear many different masks. That is why many accuse Christians of being "hypocrites". This is not how

God wants us to live. He wants us to be genuine with Him and with one another.

He doesn't want us to simply *act* like Christians. He wants us to authentically *be* Christians. The only way for this to occur is by allowing him to work on us from the inside out. It's challenging, I know!

In this life we will constantly have to choose between the world's way, tradition, or God's way.

How about you? Are you ready to live an *authentic* Christian life today? If you are, give God permission to remove the masks and trust Him with your vulnerability. If you will allow Him to work on your most inward parts, there awaits a beautiful you to be revealed. It is the genuine, authentic, *true* YOU.

Praises of the Heart

> "Praise the Lord! For it is good to sing praises to our God, for
> He is gracious *and* lovely; praise is becoming *and* appropriate.
> The Lord is building up Jerusalem; He is
> gathering together the exiles of Israel.
> He heals the brokenhearted and binds up their wounds
> [curing their pains and their sorrows]."
> (Psalm 147:1-3, AMP)

Praising God doesn't always come naturally. Especially during times of heartache, sorrow, or disappointment. Nonetheless, we should praise God in *all* things. We should praise Him regardless of our circumstance. All of creation was designed to praise Him. Witnessing a glorious sunset, observing beautiful flowers in bloom, or observing the crystal blue oceans at the beach can all evoke responses of praise. But often, it's easier to praise a sunset than the Creator of the sunset. The difficulties of life often cloud our vision and keep us from praising God. So what can we do to restore a heart-attitude of praise?

Praise, according to the Scriptures, is an act of our will that flows out of an awe and reverence for our Creator. Praise gives glory to God and opens us up to a deeper union with Him. It turns our attention off of our problems and on the nature and character of God.

As we focus our minds on God and proclaim His goodness, we reflect His glory back to Him. The results can fill you with peace and contentment (Isaiah 26:3) and transform your outlook on life.

Find a reason to praise and have a heart of gratitude even in the small things.

Very simply, we praise God because He is worthy of our praise (1 Chron. 16:25, Rev. 5:11-14). He is the Alpha and Omega, the Beginning and the

End, the King of kings and Lord of lords. He is our Creator, Provider, Healer, Redeemer, Judge, Defender and much more. If the mountains and the hills break forth before Him singing, and all the trees of the field clap their hands (Isaiah 55:12), how much more should you and I praise Him? If you *still* do not find a reason to praise God, then praise Him simply because He created and *sustains* the universe. The Lord is looking to and fro, searching for a group of people that will pause their busyness of life to give Him the praise and adoration He deserves.

Going through a hard time? Praise Him anyway. *Lost your job?* Praise Him anyway. *Health concerns?* Praise Him anyway. *Financial burdens?* Praise Him anyway. *Marital struggles?* Praise Him anyway.

Praise is the best weapon used against Satan's tactics. When we praise God, we are showing the heavenly hosts, powers and principalities, demons and angels, that our God is worthy to be praised – no matter what the circumstance.

Genuine praise must flow from the heart as an adoration towards God even during times of sorrow, discouragement, trial and temptation. The praise of His people brings glory to God as the world stands by and watches in awe; mystified as to why we still praise in the midst of seeming darkness. What a privilege it is to bring praises to our God. I can imagine it is a "sweet aroma to His nostrils" as He joyfully listens to the praises of His people.

Faith Like a Child

"At that time the disciples came up and asked Jesus, 'Who
then is [really] the greatest in the kingdom of heaven?'
And He called a little child to Himself and
put him in the midst of them,
And said, 'Truly I say to you, unless you repent (change, turn
about) and become like little children [trusting, lowly, loving,
forgiving], you can never enter the kingdom of heaven [at all].
Whoever will humble himself therefore and become like this little child
[trusting, lowly, loving, forgiving] is greatest in the kingdom of heaven.
And whoever receives *and* accepts *and* welcomes one little
child like this for My sake and in My name receives *and*
accepts *and* welcomes Me.'" (Matthew 18:1-5, AMP)

Jesus often used children as an illustration of faith and humility. Interestingly, Jesus never required that children become like adults, but that adults become like children.

So what does it mean to have "child-like" faith? Children are simple-minded. They are not contaminated by "adult-think". The special attributes of children are humility, unworldliness, simplicity, and teachableness. Whereas adults battle with being self-seeking, worldly, distrustful, conceited, and prideful. Child-like faith calls us to forsake the mentality that is so prevalent in American culture today. Faith doesn't mean that there is the absence of doubt or fear, but perseverance in spite of them.

We should enjoy observing and learning from little children. Watch them take their first few steps as they wobble their way towards mommy or daddy, trusting them every step of the way. Or observe them trying to bring a spoonful of food to their mouths, only to rejoice over the few morsels that actually made it. Or study the expression of joy that overwhelms their little faces as they are able to clap their tiny hands together over something they find humorous.

Simple-faith is grounded. That doesn't mean we reject education or intellect. It simply means we depend on God every step of the way even when we wobble through life, struggle with things we don't understand, can't seem to find our way, or fear unanswered prayers.

When God doesn't answer prayer as we want, that is where true faith begins. Let's take the struggle Jesus encountered at the Garden of Gethsemane, "My Father, if there is any way, get me out of this. But please, not what I want. You, what do *you* want?" (Matthew 26:39, MSG). There, in prayer, Jesus fought His greatest battle. As he sweat pellets of blood, He made His request known to God, yet, He trusted God for His perfect will in His life.

God did not answer Jesus' prayer on that day. He didn't rescue him from the ridicule, from the beatings, nor from the torture of hanging on a cross. He had something much MUCH greater in mind. For the salvation of mankind, and for the glory of God.

Christ points out that we must be as little children because they are the model to which the members of His kingdom must resemble themselves. Today I encourage you to move from a place of being self-sufficient into a place of being God-dependent... trusting Him every wobbly step of the way.

Pride and Prejudice

"But Naaman became angry and left. He said, 'I thought he would at least come out of his house, stand somewhere, call on the name of the Lord his God, wave his hand over the infected place, and heal the skin disease. The Abana and Pharpar Rivers in Damascus have better water than any of the rivers in Israel. Couldn't I wash in them and be clean?' So he turned around and left in anger. But Naaman's servants went to him and said, 'Master, if the prophet had asked you to do some extraordinary act, wouldn't you have done it? Why shouldn't you do as he said: 'Wash and be clean?' So he went to dip himself in the Jordan River seven times, as the man of God had instructed him. His skin became healthy again like a little child's skin. Then he and all his men returned to the man of God. Naaman stood in front of Elisha and said, 'Now I know that there's no god in the whole world, except the God of Israel. So please accept a present from me.'" (2 Kings 5:11-15, GW)

Naaman's story is so compelling because we all have struggled with pride and prejudices at one time or another. However, It's important to recognize that most of our preconceived judgements and opinions are not based on reason or actual experience at all.

Naaman was the commander of the Syrian army and had been victorious over many battles. Therefore, in his eyes, there could be no one greater than the land of Syria. He had a preconceived idea of what his healing should look like (again, never having even experienced a healing before). To add insult to injury, Elisha didn't even come to greet him at the door... he sent a messenger! I mean, didn't Elisha know what a *great* man of valor he was? Yes he did, but Elisha wasn't persuaded by the commander's title or accolades.

In reading the scripture, we can see that Naaman struggled with many prejudices. In fact, he refused to dip himself in the *dirty* rivers of Israel... after all, the waters from *his* town were much MUCH better. Had it not been for the urging of his servants, Naaman could have missed his miracle. He was so humbled by his healing (and wrong thinking) that he said, "Now I know that there's *no* god in the whole world, except the God of Israel." In essence he went from saying, "No one compares to my land" to saying "No one compares to the land of Israel".

Beloved, are there some preconceived ideas or prejudices that are hindering you from your miracle today? Take some time to reflect and allow the Holy Spirit to make this humbling story personal.

Are there any areas where you are tempted to feel superior to others?

Can you remember a time when you were guilty of pride or prejudice?

Naaman had to humble himself to listen to people he normally would have dismissed.

We all have prejudices to some extent. Sometimes it's difficult to believe we have it in us. Nonetheless, we have to deal with it and work towards humility. Perhaps the things we think we are very passionate about, whatever they may be, really stems from pride. Humbleness and humility are the keys to overcoming pride and prejudices. In doing so, we can experience more of God and make room to receive the everyday miracles God intends for our lives.

True Success

"For the love of money is a root of all evils; it is through this craving that some have been led astray and have wandered from the faith and pierced themselves through with many acute [mental] pangs."
1 Timothy 6:10 (AMP)

Many often inadvertently twist this scripture to convey that money is evil. Money is not "bad" or "evil". Money is a constant variable. Notice, it is the love of money that is evil, not "money" in itself. Before I looked up this scripture, God was showing me that when one doesn't have a healthy relationship with money, it leads to bondage. Those that think money is bad, are often bound to poverty, lacking the basic necessities of life and often needing food, clothing, and shelter. And those that love money are often bound and enticed by the world, craving many ungodly things, stray from the faith, and go through much pain (as the scripture points out).

In a world where we are on "sensory overload", it can be a difficult balance. We need to pay attention and listen to the quiet whisper of the Holy Spirit when it comes to being good stewards with God's money (did you catch that... I said, God's money). It all belongs to Him anyway.

Some may measure excellence and success by the "bottom line" - the amount of money they take home. Some "put their hope in wealth" (1 Timothy 6:17) and build their lives to accommodate that pursuit. But my hope is that you would value many things above money. Scripture teaches us that "godliness with contentment is great gain" (1 Timothy 6:6).

There is nothing wrong with being one with many accolades. Certainly teachers, firefighters, doctors and many others are vital to our society. Paul never condemned those that were wealthy, for he knew God loved to provide abundantly for His children's needs (1 Timothy 4:3-4, Eccl 5:19-20). Instead, he was concerned that they would arrogantly make riches an idol in which they trusted for security. Further, he wanted them to share with those who couldn't help themselves. But my prayer is, no matter what our profession, that at the core of our inner most being, we will know that we truly succeed by being righteous and godly people full of "faith, love, endurance and gentleness" (1 Timothy 6:11).

Dealing with Controlling People

> "There was never anyone like Ahab, who sold himself to do evil in the eyes of the LORD, urged on by Jezebel his wife. He behaved in the vilest manner by going after idols, like the Amorites the LORD drove out before Israel." (1 Kings 21:25-26)

Anytime you allow another person to redirect your plans or the destiny that God has for you, you are allowing a "Jezebel" to urge you to do that, which is contrary to the will of God. Yes, I said it, *Jezebel*. Jezebel was a wicked queen who distracted God's people from doing His will in their lives and pointed them to pagan gods. She was constantly clamoring God's chosen. She was a strong, self-willed individual who manipulated and controlled others until she had her way. Someone who operates in the same spirit as Jezebel is someone who tries to get people to do whatever they want by any means necessary without regard for what plans *God* may have for that person's life.

If you've ever had to deal with a controlling person, you know how difficult life can be while around this particular type of individual. Controlling people typically lack control in their own lives, which leaves them wanting to control the lives of others.

How do you know if you are dealing with a controlling person in your life? Here are some tips:

- They can never take *no* for an answer. If the controlling person doesn't like your response, they will ask again, repeatedly and in different forms until they get the answer they desire.
- They do not give you freedom to be *you*. Controlling people will often criticize what you do and how you do it, especially if they feel it may interfere with *their* agenda. They are also extremely critical of others

who may appear to gain more attention than they do because in their eyes, they are losing the power to influence others.
- Controlling people are not bashful about forcing their way into your life. They push themselves into your plans and before you know it, they have devised a new agenda for a plan that better suits them.
- Controlling people find it difficult to be flexible and show signs of anger when circumstances do not flow in their favor.

When dealing with these kind of individuals, I urge you to walk in the boldness and confidence that the Almighty has given you in order to do His will. If possible, disregard the Jezebel in your life. Be bold, stand your ground, and set boundaries. This does not give God's people a license to *react* but to *respond* in a godly manner while maintaining composure and confidence. Love pleasing God more than you love pleasing other people. Doing otherwise is evil in the sight of the Lord.

SPIRITUAL BULLIES

> "Listen to Me, you who know rightness *and* justice *and* right standing with God, the people in whose heart is My law *and* My instruction: fear not the reproach of men, neither be afraid *nor* dismayed at their revilings. For [in comparison with the Lord they are so weak that things as insignificant as] the moth shall eat them up like a garment, and the worm shall eat them like wool. But My rightness *and* justice [and faithfully fulfilled promise] shall be forever, and My salvation to all generations." (Isaiah 51:7-8, AMP)

We have all experienced "spiritual bullies" sometime in our lives. They can pop-up in the workplace, at school, at church, at family gatherings, or even at home. You know the type, they can do no wrong, and you can do no right. Everything you say and do is put under great scrutiny. They hide behind their assumed respectability of religion and spirituality. They feel their position, assumed skills, abilities and perception of being more enlightened than the normal person, gives them an advantage over those upon whom they prey. They are not always aware of their actions (nor could they ever conceive the thought that *they* are in fact a bully). However, these personality types can be very dangerous and damaging to believers as they levitate towards those who appear to be weaker, vulnerable, or less discerning than they are.

Just like a bull, bullies are hard and mean. They are strong-willed, belligerent, and *very* aggressive (thus the term, "bull-headed"). They can be extremely powerful in their manipulation tactics and are often, unbeknownst to them, being used as satan's tool to injure another believer by disqualifying their spiritual walk or minimizing their calling.

The enemy uses spiritual bullies to get you to start analyzing and second guessing everything you say and do. It is *then* that the enemy can paralyze you and hinder you from doing all the great things God has intended for you... fear is the crippler of a walking miracle!

Do not let spiritual bullies cripple you. We serve a God that is much *much* greater than any man (or woman) on earth. Man will eventually become dust again whereas God's salvation and promises forever stands. God's protection is so powerful that we can be protected by the mere shadow of His hand (Isaiah 51:16).

So wether you are a new believer, an old believer, or someone with or without a spiritual title, know that *you* are God's people and no spiritual bully has the power to cripple you, injure you, or paralyze you from your God-given purpose and destiny.

THE LEPROUS MAN

> "Now Naaman, captain of the army of the king of Aram, was a great man with his master, and highly respected, because by him the Lord had given victory to Aram. The man was also a valiant warrior, *but he was* a leper." (1 Kings 5:1, NASB)

Imagine for a second, being a person accomplishing many things in your life, only to be recognized for having a grotesque skin disease. As Christians, we can be recognized for doing many *many* noble things: teaching bible studies, leading prayer groups, feeding the hungry, giving to the poor, discipleship, tithing, reaching out to the community, and the like. However, if we look deep inside ourselves and our honest with ourselves, I am sure we could find many *many* ignoble things in our life.

There is a constant battle going on within our soul. We can be holy at church, but not so holy at home. We can be beautifully dressed with our Sunday best, but not so beautifully dressed in our thoughts. We can appear glorious one minute, and condemning the next. We can weep over our own sin, but find no compassion for the sin of others. We can be very sacred one minute... and the next minute - we are the *leper*.

It would be good to stare that infirmity (whatever it is) in the face and say, *"Don't you know who I am? I am chosen by the King of kings, Lord of Lords. My days have been predestined before the foundations of the earth. I am my Beloved's and He is mine."* Many may mistake that kind of talk for arrogance. But beloved, that is *confidence* in knowing who you are in HIM.

Naaman was as great as the world could make him, yet, not a single soul would want to trade skins with him. Everyone of us has a person in our life that we admire... until we know too much. Maybe *you* are the person that someone admires until they find out that...

As in Naaman's case, we all have that *"but......"* after our name or after the list of all the great things we have done or accomplished. You fill in the blank for whatever that thing is that is hindering you. Maybe it keeps us humble. Maybe without it, we would not see our need for God.

I wonder what infirmities you may be facing in your own life today? What is that one thing that keeps you from grabbing a hold of all the wonderful things that God has for you? What is that thing or things that keeps you from believing what God says about you? Maybe it is something that God wants to heal in your life, once and for all. Or maybe, just *maybe* it will be the one thing that keeps us humble and makes us so desperate for God that we rely on Him alone, *forever.*

THE STOLEN SEED

> "And I will put enmity between you and the woman, and between your offspring and her offspring; He will bruise *and* tread your head underfoot, and you will lie in wait *and* bruise His heel."
> (Genesis 3:15, AMP)

Since the beginning of time there has been an antagonist, a devious serpent, an enemy that has brought much opposition towards mankind. His seemingly victorious tactics is the result of the original fall of man. However, this scripture gives us hope in its prophecy that there would be the coming of a Savior.

In the Old Testament, "seed" is used to refer both to individual offspring and descendants in general. The woman plays a key role in being the Enemy's adversary, not because she was approached and entrapped by Satan but because she is "the mother of all living" (v. 20), for through her the Savior would come.

Although God's promise of a "seed" coming to save mankind has been fulfilled, there is still an enemy waging war against the seed of every woman. Satan *still* wants to kill, steal, and destroy generations to come. His main interest is to once again deceive women (and men) into thinking that if they will abort the seed within them, it will lead to a more prosperous life. Although Satan at times may appear cunning and clever, he is using the same old tactics and painfully, women all across the nation are allowing themselves to be deceived by Satan once again. In Genesis 3:3, Satan begins his conversation with Eve by questioning God. Eve distorted God's command by adding her own interpretation. She was exaggerating the truth to make her case appear more viable.

Today many pro-choicers justify their actions by stating, "It's my body, it's my right to choose", "Having children will leave me powerless", "I can't afford to have a child", or "I'm too young to have a baby". This is not the truth of God's word. Satan's tactic is to destroy every unborn child that they may not live to carry out their purpose and destiny here on Earth.

Right before Jesus was born, King Herod ordered that all the male babies under the age of two be killed. He feared that someone greater would become king. He did not realize that he was being used by Satan. Today many (unbeknownst to them) are being used by the Enemy to destroy innocent lives... lives that will never have the chance to fulfill their God-given destiny.

Beloved, if you or someone you know is dealing with the decision of an unplanned pregnancy, know that God has a mighty plan for this unborn's life. It takes great FAITH and COURAGE not to abort an unplanned child. But know there is a great reward for those that make the difficult decision to do the right thing.

On the other hand, if you are someone you know has suffered the guilt, shame, condemnation, judgement, pain, and loss of aborting an unplanned pregnancy; know that there is a God that wants to heal, forgive, restore, and redeem!

> *"A young pregnant wife has been hospitalized for a simple attack of appendicitis. The doctors had to apply ice to her stomach and when the treatments ended the doctors suggested that she abort the child, they told her it was the best solution because the child would be born with some disability but the young brave wife decided not to abort, and the child was born. That woman was my mother and I was the child."* - Andrea Bocelli

Toxic Relationships

> "But avoid stupid *and* foolish controversies and genealogies and dissensions and wrangling about the Law, for they are unprofitable and futile.
> [As for] a man who is factious [a heretical sectarian and cause of divisions], after admonishing him a first and second time, reject [him from your fellowship and have nothing more to do with him],
> Well aware that such a person has utterly changed (is perverted and corrupted); he goes on sinning [though he] is convicted of guilt *and* self-condemned." (Titus 3:9-11, AMP)

So *what* do toxic and unhealthy relationships look like? Toxic relationships have many faces; they pop-up with immediate and extended family members, with colleagues, in friendships, with siblings, and yes, even in church environments. Unfortunately, toxic people do not have your best interest at heart. They will rarely offer to help someone in need but will scour the earth when it is beneficial to them. Toxic people are often self-absorbed and use people repeatedly in different forms. Quite often this leaves the other person feeling hurt, taken advantage of and angry. They are consistently being brought down and often feel "used." The toxic person expects for the world to stop when they have achieved the most insignificant of accomplishments but have difficulty in celebrating those who have accomplished great things in their own lives.

Christians often feel hopelessly trapped in abusive relationships. We think the Lord wants us to be endlessly patient and tolerant of the sins of others against us. It has been engrained in us that it is sinful to protect ourselves. We often feel that it would be "un-Christian" for us to distance ourselves or to completely leave a toxic relationship. For some reason, we are under the misconception that we would not be good Christians if we did not stick it out and continue tolerating just about anything the other person says or does. But quite the opposite is true. It is "un-Christian" to allow someone to drain you to the extent that you cannot do the work God has placed in front of you. It is "un-Christian" to become so embittered by the toxic individual that you do everything with resentment. It is "un-Christian" to do whatever the toxic person wants, even if it is not what God wants for you. THAT is "un-Christian".

Abusers and their enablers pull out all the stops in trying to make us feel guilty for removing ourselves from their destructive sphere of influence. It is "Christ-like" to forgive the abuser, however, the Bible does not instruct us to continue on in an abusive relationship. In fact, the Bible tells us to have nothing to do with them (2 Timothy 3:2-5). It is important for us to establish healthy boundaries, and in doing so, we can better establish healthy relationships; removing ourselves from those that want to inflict harm or have become toxic.

Fool's Gold

"Meanwhile the crowds grew until thousands upon thousands were milling about and crushing each other. He turned now to his disciples and warned them, 'More than anything else, beware of these Pharisees and the way they pretend to be good when they aren't. But such hypocrisy cannot be hidden forever. It will become as evident as yeast in dough. Whatever they have said in the dark shall be heard in the light, and what you have whispered in the inner rooms shall be broadcast from the housetops for all to hear!'" (Luke 12:1-5, TLB)

When I was a young girl, my father surprised me with a sweet treasure. As I opened my hand, my brown eyes widened in amazement when he handed me a *gold* nugget! I couldn't help but gawk at the sparkling sight. It shined in all its brilliant array. I often kept it by my bedside just so I could admire its "glitter" until I fell asleep.

However, as I grew older and was able to understand things a little more, I realized what my dad had handed me was *not* a gold nugget at all… it was *fool's gold*.

Don't get me wrong, I still valued the thoughtful treasure my dad had given me as a little girl; but as I matured, I began to understand the difference between the counterfeit and the *real deal*. On the outside, both the real gold and the fool's gold appear to be the same. But indeed, they are both *very* different. The fact is, real gold can be worth over $1,700 per ounce, while you'll be lucky to get a buck for that much pyrite (fool's gold).

One way to be able to tell the difference between real gold and the fake stuff is to put the minerals through a "streak test". When rubbed against a streak plate, the minerals true colors are revealed. REAL gold leaves behind a vibrant yellow color that's highly reflective to the surrounding light. Pyrite typically leaves behind a dark black powder.

My point? I wonder how many of us could distinguish the real thing from the counterfeit? I wonder how many of us, when rubbed the wrong way, will be like pure gold, leaving behind the brilliant light of Jesus Christ? Or maybe, we are more like fool's gold, revealing the true heart by leaving behind a trail of "dark" stuff (ouch)!

In a world of Instagram, Snapchat, and Facebook, it is really easy to portray the lie we want people to believe about us. People confuse a picture that can be produced in a second for a life that is seemingly "perfect".

It takes bold and courageous Christians to be vulnerable. The world is waiting for believers that are willing to lay down their pride, their status quo, and their seemingly perfect christianity for authenticity... *that's what's real*. Be truthful, it leads to freedom. That's what leaves God's brilliance behind. Yes, it will cost us. It may cost us some pride, maybe our friends, and maybe our social status or position. But we will gain the world for Jesus.

Today I challenge every believer to be brave enough to just go there and BE REAL. Living a life of falsehood leads to bondage, but living a life of authenticity leads to freedom (not only yours, but those watching). So let us do some heart searching and ask ourselves this very hard and vulnerable question, "Am I the real deal... like pure gold? Or I'm I inauthentic... like fools gold?"

Prosper Even as Your Soul Prospers

"Beloved, I pray that you may prosper in every way and [that your body] may keep well, even as [I know] your soul keeps well *and* prospers." (3 John 1:2, AMP)

What does it mean to have a soul that *prospers*? The three parts of mankind is the body, soul, and spirit. The body is the physical make-up of an individual whereas the soul houses the mind, will, and emotions. In essence, the soul houses the heart. Proverbs declares, "Watch over your **heart** with all diligence, for from it flow the wellsprings of life." (Proverbs 4:23). We see here that the heart is central to our emotions and will. To prosper simply means to succeed. Most people automatically envision to "prosper" means to succeed monetarily. Although, John specifically states that he desires us to prosper in *every* way, he specifically pointed out that it is important for our bodies and our souls to succeed (in contrast to failing us).

Can you envision what God's people could accomplish here on earth if we had prosperous bodies and souls? When we read the story of Esther, we see that she was on a mission to win the King's heart to save her people. Esther trusted God and walked by faith every step of the way to accomplish her mission. However, God was preparing her long before she began to walk into her mission!

What is a poor body, poor soul, poor health and poor habits keeping us from? What has God called us to do that we are failing to accomplish because we are always sick, tired, and emotional?

If that is you today, there is still hope! First, you must build a firm foundation. Never try to build a house without first laying a foundation. Take the time to work on your body, soul, spirit, and heart. God has given us the tools we need through His Word. If you don't have a firm foundation, that "house" will be so unstable it will soon come tumbling down.

That's especially true in the area of prosperity. Often, people are so desperate for a "quick fix", that they do whatever the latest trend is, without seeking God and allowing Him to change anything else in their lives. Of course, it doesn't work and those people end up disappointed. Sometimes they even come to the conclusion that it wasn't God's will for them to prosper after all.

I encourage you all to spend time in prayer and in God's Word today, seeking His will for your life because He *does* want you to succeed and prosper... even as your soul prospers! How are you going to affect God's kingdom today?

Law vs Grace

"But when Peter came to Antioch I had to oppose him publicly, speaking strongly against what he was doing, for it was very wrong. For when he first arrived, he ate with the Gentile Christians who don't bother with circumcision and the many other Jewish laws. But afterwards, when some Jewish friends of James came, he wouldn't eat with the Gentiles anymore because he was afraid of what these Jewish legalists, who insisted that circumcision was necessary for salvation, would say; and then all the other Jewish Christians and even Barnabas became hypocrites too, following Peter's example, though they certainly knew better." (Galatians 2:11-13, TLB)

Peter preached the gospel to the Jews, while Paul worked among the Gentiles. Instead of criticizing one another for our differences, Paul gives a great example of working together to spread the gospel to *all* people. His frustration with Peter was *not* that he was dining with Gentiles (the seemingly less spiritual crowd), but that he would hide his relationship with them because of fear of what the Jewish (the seemingly more spiritual crowd) would think!

The Gentiles didn't practice all the Laws the Jewish leaders were careful to obtain. Nevertheless, Paul stated that an individual is not justified by the Law but by faith in Jesus alone (v. 16). He further states that no one will *ever* be justified by works. We are justified through Christ, freely being righteous by our faith. Yet still, why are there so many believers striving to do a bunch of works to earn God's good graces? Whatever we do for the Lord, should it not be out of love rather than obligation? Many believers know the Law all too well but know nothing about the beauty of God's grace. Here are a few ways to recognize if you are living under the Law or under God's grace:

- The Law is based on works vs Grace is based on faith

- The Law shows us how to earn our way to Christ vs Grace shows us we are heirs with Christ
- The Law condemns us vs Grace frees us

Many who do a good job of keeping the Law condemn those that do not (as with the Jews and Gentiles). You can often recognize when someone is trying to condemn you because they express ill thoughts of you and pronounce judgement against you (placing themselves as equals with God). They investigate you and make a wrongful decision about you based on the Law. Condemnation is accusatory which comes from the enemy. One's condemning heart is often revealed when they try to place others in bondage due to the Law.

Grace expresses God's loving-kindness towards us. In grace we can experience God's goodwill and the joy that comes from being free from the debt of sin. God's favor and generosity is a *free* gift to us.

Which one will you choose today?

Gathering with the Brethren

"So let's *do* it—full of belief, confident that we're presentable inside and out. Let's keep a firm grip on the promises that keep us going. He always keeps his word. Let's see how inventive we can be in encouraging love and helping out, not avoiding worshiping together as some do but spurring each other on, especially as we see the big Day approaching." (Hebrews 10:22-25, MSG)

To "worship together" or to "fellowship" describes the beautiful relationship of faith which connects Christians to God and to one another. Yet, in the religious world, not only among denominations but among our own brethren this word is used to reference everything from recreation halls built onto church meeting houses, to casual social interaction between Christians and non-Christians.

The word "fellowship" in the Greek is *koinonia*. It simply means, in association with, community, communion, joint participation" (*Greek-English Lexicon of the New Testament,* p. 352). Scripture commands a powerful example of what koinonia should look like: be devoted to one another, honor one another, live in harmony with one another, accept one another, serve one another, be kind and compassionate to one another, admonish one another, encourage one another, spur one another on toward love and good deeds, offer hospitality, and love one another. THIS is what true biblical koinonia (or fellowship) should look like.

So often, when believers are gathered together, there appears to be "a right of passage" to "pick apart" or be critical of one another's shortcomings. This is not true fellowship. Remember, the primary purpose for gathering together and fellowshipping is to magnify Christ and encourage one another, not scrutinize one another.

It is a *great* thing to come together and worship and fellowship with other believers at church on Sundays, however, this is not the *only* way or the *only* time to have fellowship. Fellowshipping with other believers can take place anywhere that God resides (and if you are a believer today, this includes anywhere *you* are). This can take place at a home, at a restaurant, at your workplace, or in the parking lot! God is not confined by the brick and mortar of our church walls.

To have true fellowship, believers should gather together having one spiritual goal in mind... to glorify God. Believers should gather together and be called together as being led by the Holy Spirit. Without the leading of the Holy Spirit, we are just a bunch of people gathering together for another social event... this is *not* fellowshipping, this is socializing.

Today I encourage you to gather with another believer (or two) and fellowship wherever you are. Paying special attention to the scripture mentioned above and encouraging one another in love.

Bearing Good Fruit

"I am the True Vine, and My Father is the Vinedresser.
Any branch in Me that does not bear fruit [that stops bearing]
He cuts away (trims off, takes away); and He cleanses *and*
repeatedly prunes every branch that continues to bear fruit,
to make it bear more *and* richer *and* more excellent fruit.
You are cleansed *and* pruned already, because of the word which
I have given you [the teachings I have discussed with you].
Dwell in Me, and I will dwell in you. [Live in Me, and I will live in you.]
Just as no branch can bear fruit of itself without abiding in (being vitally
united to) the vine, neither can you bear fruit unless you abide in Me.
I am the Vine; you are the branches. Whoever lives in Me and
I in him bears much (abundant) fruit. However, apart from Me
[cut off from vital union with Me] you can do nothing.
If a person does not dwell in Me, he is thrown out like a [broken-off] branch, and withers; such branches are gathered up and
thrown into the fire, and they are burned. (John 15:1-6, AMP)

Every year we go through a season of harsh, bitter winters. Albeit, some winters are harsher than others. Particularly after a heavy snowfall, it is not uncommon to see broken-off tree branches in yards and throughout neighborhoods. These branches are useless. Since they do not burn well, they cannot even be used to warm a house. They are thrown into piles and burned like garbage. They can no longer bear any "fruit" (nor bloom with greenery or beautiful flowers) because it has been "cut-off" from the main vine.

In the same manner, Jesus is the "true" vine and every believer must abide (live or remain) in Him. Believers are the "branches" of God's vine and can do nothing, nor bear *good* fruit apart from Him. To put it simply, without Him, we are of no good use. However *with* Christ, the "fruit" we see is God's expression of power working inwardly. We can see the power of God in those who are brought into a living union with Christ and the product is "the fruit of the Spirit" (Galatians 5:22-23).

The Vinedresser's pruning knife is the Word of God. God's Word cleans the sin out of our lives. It supernaturally transforms us. That stimulates fruitfulness. Sometimes the Father uses the harsh, bitter seasons of our life to make us more responsive to His Word. Most of us become more sensitive to the truth of Scripture when we are in *need* of Him. When we have a particular problem, scripture will often seem to leap off the page. It is often through the painful seasons of our life that the Word of God comes alive. And those who overcome and remain, even through the coldness of life, will get to experience the beauty of the next season to come.

Charles Spurgeon once said, *"The Word is often the knife with which the great Husbandman prunes the vine; and, brothers and sisters, if we were more willing to feel the edge of the Word, and to let it cut away something that may be very dear to us, we should not need so much pruning by affliction. It is because that first knife does not always produce the desired result that another sharp tool is used by which we are effectually pruned."*

The pruning process helps us bear more fruit. If there is no fruit in your life, if there is no genuine connection to Jesus Christ, if you are not truly saved, then you are in real danger of being removed and cast into the fire forever. If there is fruit in you life, you can rejoice that affliction is making the pruning knife more effective, and that the Vinedresser's ultimate goal is that you bear much fruit.

Celebrate

"When Mordecai learned what had been done, he ripped his clothes to shreds and put on sackcloth and ashes. Then he went out in the streets of the city crying out in loud and bitter cries. He came only as far as the King's Gate, for *no one dressed in sackcloth was allowed to enter the King's Gate.* As the king's order was posted in every province, there was loud lament among the Jews—fasting, weeping, wailing. And most of them stretched out on sackcloth and ashes."
(Esther 4:1-3, MSG)

I was so humbled by the above scripture and the revelation that came with it. In biblical times, Jews often wore sackcloth to depict a fatal sickness, trouble, deep sorrow, or death.

But *today,* Christians all over the world can *remove* that sackcloth of mourning and *rejoice* in clothes of victory! As Christians, this is the celebration that comes with the resurrected hope of Jesus Christ. The foundation of a Christian's belief is that we too will rise again in eternal life with Him when we receive Jesus Christ as our Lord and Savior.

"Why do you look for the living among the dead? He is not there; he has risen!"
(Luke 24:5)

Christian or not, we often see pics of the crucifixion almost everywhere we go. The symbol of the cross is worn around people's necks as jewelry. We see it on hats and t-shirts as fashion statements. One popular fashion designer couples the cross with that of a skull. (Seems ironic considering the cross came to abolish death, not dwell among it). But Jesus's crucifixion is only part of the story.....

We see in the above scripture that those who wear sackcloth cannot enter into the King's Gate. If Jesus dying on the cross was where it began and where it ended, Christians all over the world would still be wearing sackcloths today. Similarly to the above scripture, we would have *no access* to our KING. We would still be mourning the death of a powerless Savior.

But *now*, because of the POWER of Jesus' and HIS resurrection, we can REMOVE the sackcloth of mourning, CLOTH ourselves in strength and victory, and enter into THE KING'S Gate. We can talk with Him, dine with Him, pray to Him, have fellowship with Him, have one on one intimacy with Him, and reign with Him... *forever.* Do you see it? THAT, ladies and gentlemen, is the good news of the gospel! Furthermore, we don't have to wait until we die to have full access to Him, we can have full access to him *now*.

Beloved, be encouraged. The hope of Jesus' resurrection and our access to Him and the ability to have communion with Him is still ALIVE. Now that's something worth celebrating!

God vs Idols

"To whom can God be compared? How can you describe what he is like? He is not like an idol that workers make, that metalworkers cover with gold and set in a base of silver." (Isaiah 40:18-19, GNT)

In this scripture, Isaiah is proclaiming the majesty of God over all other idols (or man-made images). No one or *nothing* can compare to the Creator of Heaven and Earth. No one can instruct The Lord; He is an all-knowing God.

The prophet appears to make a mockery of those that would even suggest comparing the Creator to any other image.

Today there are various forms of idolatry, having one motive in common: "self". Although we no longer bow down to idols and images, modern idolatry can take various forms.

First, we worship at the altar of materialism. "Keeping up with the Jones'" is not a phrase that is confined to just the non-believer but many believers fall into this form of idolatry as well. There is nothing wrong with Christians having nice things (in fact, scripture is filled with the many blessings God had given His people). However, believers seem to have lost their way and sight of the fact that the focus must always be on God *first*, not material possession.

Second, we worship at the altar of our own pride and ego. This often takes the form of obsession with careers, jobs, titles, and acting "busy". The busier someone can pretend they are, the more they can fulfill their self-worth and need to feel important. In the meantime, children are starving for love and attention, marriages are dwindling, and godly relationships become nonexistent. All of this "is meaningless and a great misfortune. What does a man get for all the toil and anxious striving with which he labors under the sun? All his days his work is pain and grief; even at night his mind does not rest. This too is meaningless" (Ecclesiastes 2:21-23).

Third, we idolize man. Especially, those with riches or powerful titles. We have all seen this type of idolatry…people going out of their way to do seemingly "good works" to be noticed by the pastor or boss but pays no mind to the homeless, the widow, or the broken. But if we are a people truly living holy lives, we would worship the Lord and Savior alone, not man, position, or their titles.

Our hearts and minds must be centered around Christ. This is why when asked what is the greatest commandment, Jesus replied, "Love the Lord your God with all your heart and with all your soul and with all your mind" (Matthew 22:37). When we love the Lord with everything that is in us, there will be no room in our hearts for idolatry.

New Covenant

"But this is the promise that I will make to Israel after those days, says the Lord: I will put my teachings inside them, and I will write those teachings on their hearts. I will be their God, and they will be my people. No longer will each person teach his neighbors or his relatives by saying, 'Know the Lord.' All of them from the least important to the most important will all know me because I will forgive their wickedness and I will no longer hold their sins against them." (Hebrews 8:10-12, GW)

Throughout the year, we have the opportunity to celebrate various holidays. With every celebration, our minds our flooded with all sorts of emotions. Some good, some bad. Some of us made good choices and some of us... not so good choices. These memories and choices are forever engraved in our minds which can provoke various thoughts and feelings. Although we may never know the reasoning behind all that has occurred in our lives, memories filled with pain can begin to heal when we ask God to help us see from His heavenly perspective... *just as the Heavens are above the Earth, so are my ways higher than your ways and my thoughts higher than your thoughts* (Isaiah 55:9).

Every waking day we have the opportunity to choose to forgive those who have victimized us and to repent of any of our own sins. As the wounds of painful memories dig deep, we can bring our feelings to God for healing. The old adage, *Time heals all wounds* is certainly true and over a period of time, God can lessen the pain if we are patient as He does a work within us. God can replace pain, disappointments, rejection, and discouragement with healing, hope, love, acceptance, tenderness, and encouragement.

Christ alone is the answer to having a *new* covenant with God and moving past the things of old. The introduction of the "new" means that all things of "old" must be replaced. The New Covenant provides forgiveness for past (and future) sins.

God does not completely erase the memories of the past. They are advantageous in that we learn and grow from them. He can however, alter our perspective and helps us to move forward everyday with courage and victory in greater wholeness.

Out of the Cage of Religion

"The wicked are edgy with guilt, ready to
run off even when no one's after them; Honest people are
relaxed and confident, bold as lions. (Proverbs 28:1, MSG)
"The lion, which is mightiest among beasts and turns
not back before any." (Proverbs 30:30, AMP)

While visiting the local zoo, one might be surprised to see the lion quietly domiciled within its cage. We may even find it gently licking its paws or taking a little cat nap. In fact, if we didn't know better, we could think that the lion was as harmless as one of our domesticated sweet, gentle, furry household pets. However, the lion is one of great power and passion and its strength and boldness is recognized throughout the world. This can be deceiving because while in its cage, the lion does not have room to exude the true power and authority it was created for. These traits are only revealed while out in the open, on the hunt, while stalking prey, or confronting an adversary.

The lion is not unlike many believers caged in churches today. Many religious circles enforce the facade that Christians are supposed to dress a certain way, act a certain way, or smile a certain way. "Religion" is consumed with all the external aspects. Especially when it comes to ceremonies or traditions of man (which many times is unbiblical and done purely out of habitual practices). It is unreal and deceptive. *Pure* religion, however, is looking after the orphan, the widow, the community (James 1:26-27). It is about a pure relationship with Christ and doing all things in obedience to Him... not to receive praises from men (John 12:43). Religion is careful to stay within the confines of external appearances of men's services. All the while, robbing believers of the power and authority Christ came to give every one of His children. The result is a domesticated and defeated church body. It is God's intent for every believer to walk in power and passion and strength and boldness that all may recognize Him throughout the world!

As Christians, we should always be walking in a biblical boldness. We should be confident in speaking truth in *love* (not out of arrogance, pride, or judgement) because we carry Christ in us. Speaking such truth in love makes God's presence known and felt. Boldness does not mean being obnoxious or having a harsh and aggressive personality. This type of character does not draw people towards the Lord but makes people want to run *away* from Him. Our motivation should not be based on proving that we are always right but our motivation should be for the salvation of individual souls. This kind of boldness is something we should ask God to receive (otherwise it is futile works done out of the pride of our flesh).

Submission, humbleness, humility, and boldness should work *together* (not as opposing characteristics). Godly boldness is found in an unwavering security and confidence in the Lord and kept within the boundaries God has set. A believer can stand for what is right even in the face of overwhelming adversity and receive God's favor and blessings.

Sanctified for a Purpose

> "Before I formed you in the womb, I knew you; Before you were born I sanctified you; I ordained you a prophet to the nations." (Jeremiah 1:5, NKJV)

God's call on Jeremiah's existence was ordained even before his birth. The above scripture illustrates the extent to which God was active in Jeremiah's life, preparing him for a destiny and a purpose that only he could fulfill in his lifetime.

"Sanctified" (Heb. qadash) reveals a people that are set apart for God's purpose. Even before our formation in the womb, God knew us. He predestined a sovereign purpose for our lives and set us apart for His special use.

Jeremiah felt ill equipped to fulfill God's purpose for his life due to his age (v. 6). He was quick to point out all of his inadequacies and downfalls, not much unlike Moses (Exodus 3:11, 4:10-13), and not much unlike many of us today.

God has plans for you and I in this lifetime. God spoke to Jeremiah through the ordinary experiences of life and He desires to do the same with us today. I encourage you to open your hearts to hear His voice in everyday ordinary experiences that He may reveal to you your purpose and destiny. For without vision, God's people perish. (Proverbs 29:18).

Spiritual Slumber

"The Lord has made you drowsy, ready to fall into a deep sleep. The prophets should be the eyes of the people, but God has blindfolded them. The meaning of every prophetic vision will be hidden from you; it will be like a sealed scroll. If you take it to someone who knows how to read and ask him to read it to you, he will say he can't because it is sealed. If you give it to someone who can't read and ask him to read it to you, he will answer that he doesn't know how. The Lord said, 'These people claim to worship me, but their words are meaningless, and their hearts are somewhere else. Their religion is nothing but human rules and traditions, which they have simply memorized. So I will startle them with one unexpected blow after another. Those who are wise will turn out to be fools, and all their cleverness will be useless.'" (Isaiah 29:10-14, GNT)

It is not uncommon for God's people to absorb the traditions of religion, go through all the motions, and yet have hearts that are far away from Him. When this occurs, it is very possible for an individual (although once spiritual), to fall into the pit of spiritual slumber. It is not part of God's plan for His people to be deaf and blind towards the prompting of His spirit. It is not God's desire for godly men to fear other men and succumb to *their* commands when it overrides God's commands. The result is a lack of personal experience with God in the lives of God's people, a condition compared to deep sleep (v. 10). However, this is inevitable when hearts begin to separate themselves from intimacy with Him.

So how does a believer break away from this "spiritual slumber"? Here are just a few ways:

1.) It is always good to seek godly counsel, however, it is vital for a believer to have a personal experience by seeking God FIRST

2.) Have a heart of obedience towards The Lord. We don't have to understand it, get man's approval for it, distrust it, or question it... just obey!
3.) Use the Word of God as a mirror, a reflection of your heart, and ask Him to remove anything that hinders you from a more personal and intimate relationship with Him.

Disobedience, disappointments, hopelessness, discouragement, and weariness are all but a few experiences that can lead one to "give up" and give way to spiritual slumber. I encourage you, no matter what you are going through today, don't give up! My prayer for those that have fallen into the spirit of deep sleep is to awake and arise and fulfill the perfect plan and destiny God has purposed for your lives!

Fruit Inspectors

"Along the way, watch out for false prophets. They will come to you in sheep's clothing, but underneath *that quaint and innocent wool,* they are hungry wolves. But you will recognize them by their fruits. You don't find *sweet, delicious* grapes growing on thorny bushes, do you? You don't find *delectable* figs growing in the midst of *prickly* thistles. *People and their lives are like trees.* Good trees bear beautiful, tasty fruit, but bad trees bear ugly, bitter fruit. A good tree cannot bear ugly, bitter fruit; nor can a bad tree bear fruit that is beautiful and tasty. And what happens to the rotten trees? They are cut down. They are used for firewood. *When a prophet comes to you and preaches this or that,* look for his fruits: *sweet or sour? rotten or ripe?*" (Matthew 7:15-20, Voice)

Many believers use the above scripture to mean to be judgmental and critical of everyone that comes our way, particularly the brethren. However, in the beginning of this chapter God forewarns, "Judge not, that you be not judged. For with what judgement you judge, you will be judged; and with the measure you use, it will be measured back to you. And why do you look at the speck in your brother's eye, but not consider the plank in your own eye?" (Matthew 7:1-3). God knew many would misinterpret the above scripture, causing more harm than good, therefore warning against such temptations to judge.

However, what the above scripture is saying, is for believers to *discern* what is truth and what is not. Christians should inspect their own fruit first and foremost, scrutinizing ourselves with careful examination, determining our own faults. Once we examine ourselves, we can discern others fallacies and steer clear of them. Even so, once we become inspectors of ourselves and see our own shortcomings, we will see that God alone is worthy to be Judge.

To *judge,* according to the Vine's dictionary, is "one who functions as judge and jury" or "arrogates to himself" (Thomas Nelson, 2005). God alone is the Judge of His people. When we as believers judge, we are placing ourselves *above* that individual and more importantly, above God. We must not judge our brother and assume such an authority over others. The Bible clearly states to be *"subject to one another. Be not many masters"* (James 3:1).

To *discern*, according to the Vine's dictionary, is to pay attention to "what is of the Holy Spirit" or distinguishing what is "of evil or of God" (Thomas Nelson, 2005). God wants us to be careful in recognizing and discerning the truth from the lie. Discern fruits, not gifts. Discernment is not a case for judgement. This statement may sound conflicting however through self examination, prayer, and guidance through the Holy Spirit, we are able to build the bridge between the two passages.

God directs us in how to conduct ourselves in reference to the faults of others and His expression frowns upon the scribes and Pharisees, who were very rigid, severe, and condemning. They were proud and conceited in justifying themselves (Matthew 23). Now, do we as believers want to be as the Pharisees?

We must not sit in the judgment-seat, to make our word a law to every body. We must not judge our brother, that is, we must not *speak evil* of him. We must not make the worst of people. We must not judge the hearts of others, nor their intentions, for it is God's place to test the heart.

If we presume to judge others, we must expect to be ourselves judged. He who places himself on the authoritative bench, shall be called to the bar of harsher judgement. No mercy shall be shown to the reputation of those that show no mercy to the reputation of others. Yet that is not the worst of it, they shall be judged of God and from Him they shall receive the *greater condemnation* (James 3:1).

EARTHLY RICHES

> "And Jesus said to His disciples, 'Truly I say to you, it will be difficult for a rich man to get into the kingdom of heaven. Again I tell you, it is easier for a camel to go through the eye of a needle than for a rich man to go into the kingdom of heaven.' When the disciples heard this, they were utterly puzzled (astonished, bewildered), saying, 'Who then can be saved [from eternal death]?' But Jesus looked at them and said, 'With men this is impossible, but all things are possible with God.'"
> (Matthew 19:23-26, AMP)

The Jews often interpreted wealth as a sign of God's blessings and a sure ticket to heaven. Instead, Jesus used this illustration to demonstrate that wealth, if not handled properly and with a pure heart, can be dangerous. He explained that with great wealth comes great responsibility. He was zoning in on the fact that very few are able to handle wealth properly, often forsaking God's call on their life for earthly possessions. However, Jesus was not condemning wealthy people. In fact, the Bible illustrates how the Israelites (God's people) were materially blessed above all the people of the earth. Abraham was made righteous by His belief in God and was very wealthy (Genesis 13:2). God had an "everlasting covenant" with Isaac and he was considered wealthy. We have the examples of people like Jacob, David, Solomon, Joseph who were all very rich men but were still able to put God first, before their riches. Jesus' statement was not to condemn but to teach the Jews that true salvation comes from God alone.

The call to forsake everything and follow Jesus is a call to put God first in all things. Money or having wealth is not sinful, however, it is the *love* of money that causes one to sin (idolatry). The amazement of the disciples is based on the assumption that riches were always a sign of God's blessing and favor (which is what a lot of "prosperity preachers" still teach today). Money can be a good thing when appropriated properly as led by the

Holy Spirit. With money we can feed the poor and the hungry, we can give to the homeless shelter, we can give to our churches, we can fund missionaries, we can build an orphanage, and so on.

Whether poor or rich, we all have a responsibility to abandon all in obedience to Christ first and foremost. God's favor and blessings on our life are not established by how many earthly goods we have (consider Job, Mary and Joseph, Jesus)! We are not to be consumed by material possessions nor hindered or bound by them. Whatever we have, whether little or great, may we be consumed with being obedient to Christ, even if that means giving all that we have for the sake of the Kingdom of Christ.

MANIPULATION

> "One final word of counsel, friends. Keep a sharp eye out for those who take bits and pieces of the teaching that you learned and then use them to make trouble. Give these people a wide berth. They have no intention of living for our Master Christ. They're only in this for what they can get out of it, and aren't above using pious sweet talk to dupe unsuspecting innocents."
> (Romans 16:17-18, MSG)

Paul describes those that are divisive as selfish and "sweet talkers". God desires peace, unity, and harmony amongst His people. However, we must refrain from (and guard our hearts against) being manipulated (or being the manipulator) in *every* area of our lives. Most of the time, master manipulators do not even realize that they are walking in a demonic spirit of manipulation because they are operating out of their fears and insecurities.... it is just their way of life. The manipulator's goal is to control your feelings, thoughts, and behaviors. Christian Counselor Leslie Vernick states, *"They want to get what they want regardless of what it costs you. They often use multiple combinations of these techniques, but the most common ones are:*

1. *Guilt tripping or making you feel bad about your own feelings, thoughts and needs*
2. *Crying, acting dependent, despondent, sulking, withdrawing*
3. *Name calling, personal attacks, criticism*
4. *Pleading, begging and repeating something over and over and over again until you wear down"*

The manipulator is constantly on "survival-mode" and their mind is often consumed with thoughts of, "I know my way is better", "I deserve this", or "I am going to do whatever I need to do to get what I want". This kind of control trusts in oneself instead of trusting in God's sovereign plan for each individual's life. Most manipulators fear that if they don't work hard enough to take control of their lives, they will somehow get the "short end of the stick". Manipulation is rooted in pride and selfishness. Going to extremities to make sure others have a high view of them, no matter who they hurt along the way. You can spot someone who is a manipulator because they view others as objects. The manipulated often feel as though they are "choking" because what the manipulator seeks to do is to restrain one's freedom by means of control. Manipulators will use tools of power, deception, position, and distortion as a means to control. The result, even if perceived as successful will never be long-lasting as the individual believes they know more than God.

However, *healthy* people find ways to compromise and respect one another's differences, feelings and desires. A manipulator pushes and pressures to get his/her own way by ignoring another person's needs and will try to make the other person feel guilty by making statements like, "You're so selfish" or try to intimidate others by making them afraid so that the other person will give in and give them what they want.

Sarah manipulated her husband Abraham into laying with her maidservant Hagar. The result? Sarah became embittered and later regretted her decision to manipulate.

Rebekah manipulated her husband Isaac into blessing their younger son, Jacob in lieu of his twin brother Esau. The result? Jacob and Esau had a strained relationship for over 20 years.

Although it may seem successful for a moment, nothing good comes out of manipulation. The end result is often devastating. The temptation to manipulate shows a lack of trust in God and suggests that God is not doing the right thing, thus, taking matters into ones own hands. Manipulators strive to control their environment, circumstances, and people by whatever means possible. Ultimately, manipulation is a deep seeded root of insecurity that manifests itself in a driving desire for the need to control.

Wisdom Beyond Years

> "But the godly will flourish like palm trees and
> grow strong like the cedars of Lebanon.
> For they are transplanted to the Lord's own
> house. They flourish in the courts of our God.
> Even in old age they will still produce fruit; they
> will remain vital and green.
> They will declare, 'The Lord is just! He is my
> rock! There is no evil in him!'"
> (Psalm 92:12-15, NLT)

Aging is often one of the hardest seasons in life to have to go through. Hair starts graying or thinning, the scale starts changing, and bones start creaking. However, the Bible reassures us that we can be completely secure in God's hand, even while going through the aging-process. Looks, health, and circumstances change with time, often in ways that are undesirable.

Many try to cope with aging by trying to cling to outward beauty, youthful strength, or various achievements. Yet, only when recognizing that growing old is part of God's plan is one able to embrace this new season of life. Although opportunities and abilities appear to decline, one must be confident in knowing that growing old is *still* part of God's perfect plan for every person's life. God's plan includes people of *every* age. Sure, life may start to look differently, however, we should not confuse change with punishment for becoming geriatric. Those who live each day for Christ will bear great fruit not only in youth but in old age as well.

God's Word does not change with the whims of our culture or society. Therefore, His word still stands true therein which the elderly should be respected (Leviticus 19:32). On the other hand, this does not mean that there is not something that the younger can teach to the *older* (1 Timothy 4:12, 1 John 2:13-14). It takes true wisdom, a heart of humility, and maturity for one to recognize that there is much to be gained from the younger generation. God's plan is for the young and old to work together for His purposes.... both in submission unto God.

In the Bible, old age is considered the positive and good fulfillment of a life devoted to God. Both the blessings and responsibilities of aging are to be accepted with gratitude and with a sense of stewardship. All the while being confident in knowing that there is a place for the older generation that is still vital for the church to properly function today.

Setting Up a Monument

> "Then the word of the Lord came to Samuel, saying,
> 'I regret making Saul king, for he has turned back from following Me and has not performed My commands.' And Samuel was grieved *and* angry [with Saul], and he cried to the Lord all night. When Samuel rose early to meet Saul in the morning, he was told, Saul came to Carmel, and behold, he set up for himself a monument or trophy [of his victory] and passed on and went down to Gilgal.
> (1 Samuel 15:10-12, AMP)

A "monument" is used for the sole purpose of making an individual or event famous. It is quite often used to attract attention, gain notoriety, gain attention, recognition and notability.

However, God's people should not strive to make themselves famous. We should bring notoriety to Christ and Christ alone. We must also be guarded against hiding behind the masks of special titles, or ministry names; appearing to do the work of the Lord but wrongfully trying to use the name of the Lord to make *oneself* known. A good litmus test is if we find ourselves talking more about OURSELVES, OUR good works, OUR business, OUR church, and OUR ministry, then we are definitely off "kilter". We have lost our focus. We are off balance. We are out of order, confused, muddled, disoriented, out of tune, out of whack, discombobulated and out of step with God. The result of performing for self-notification will ultimately lead to failure. It cannot be expressed enough that when believers lose focus on Christ and start to focus on *self*, we are treading on dangerous waters. After all, wasn't satan casted into hell because he too thought of himself more highly than he ought? Even seeing himself more valuable then God?

Believers should make a conscious effort to avoid building up a monument for themselves, especially guarding against building a monument in our own hearts. Let The Lord promote you. Let others admonish and compliment you. It is more valuable than if we promote and boast about ourselves. When individuals strive for recognition, uplift themselves, and boast constantly, they are revealing insecurities and their words carry no weight. They truly do not know who they are in Christ because if they did, they would boast on Christ alone!

Interestingly, in v. 15 we see where Saul makes excuses for disobeying The Lord and blamed others by saying, "the PEOPLE spared the best sheep and oxen, to sacrifice to The Lord your God..." Case in point, hiding behind the mask of, "We are doing all this for The Lord!" In the end we learn that The Lord *rejected* Saul because of his actions and gave his kingdom (ministry, business, church) to someone else (v. 28).

RADICAL CHRISTIANITY

"In those days John the Baptist came preaching in the wilderness of Judea, and saying, 'Repent, for the kingdom of heaven is at hand!' For this is he who was spoken of by the prophet Isaiah, saying: 'The voice of one crying in the wilderness: 'Prepare the way of the Lord; Make His paths straight.' Now John himself was clothed in camel's hair, with a leather belt around his waist; and his food was locusts and wild honey. Then Jerusalem, all Judea, and all the region around the Jordan went out to him and were baptized by him in the Jordan, confessing their sins." (Matthew 3:1-6, NKJV)

John the Baptist was one of the most distinctive characters of the New Testament. Even during biblical times, he was accused of being too "radical". He was often misunderstood because it wasn't the "norm" to walk around proclaiming the Lord, every minute, day in and day out. It wasn't the "norm" to wear camel's hair and to have locusts and honey as a scrumptious meal. But something we must understand about John is that he was called to be a forerunner... a leader for his generation.

John clearly understood his mission in life and knew he was set apart by God for a distinctive purpose. I find it interesting that despite all of John's oddities, "all the region went out to him". His radical obedience to God and his love for the coming Messiah drew many to him. The result? Many repented and were baptized. Jesus himself stated, "Among them that are born of women, there has not arisen a greater one than John the Baptist..." (Mt. 11:11). This is the greatest compliment anyone could have, coming from the greatest man that ever walked this earth. I am sure that John's radical obedience moved the heart of God.

It isn't radical Christianity to hear the Holy Spirit and to obey it. This should be "Christianity 101". It isn't radical Christianity to pay your tithe (this is done out of obedience). Radical Christianity is standing on the root of God's truths, even if it opposes traditional "churchianity". Radical Christianity is taking personal action and obeying Christ, no matter what the cost. Radical Christianity can change social order, maybe even "church order" if God is requiring a deeper spiritual intimacy within the congregation. Radical Christianity is forsaking the comforts of Western civilization (IF God calls you to).

Radical Christians start movements of revival for their generation (which begins with repentance in that individual's heart *first*). Many fear "radical Christianity" because it may require walking in an obedience that is out of the norm. However, God uses the ordinary and makes it extraordinary when we are in radical obedience to Him.

On the flip side, many well-meaning teachers want us to believe that following Christ genuinely requires sacrifice, inconvenience, being uncomfortable, and will *cost us*. I have seen many trying to do things "in the name of Christ", only to become weary, bitter, oppressed and depressed to the extent of nearly having a psychological breakdown. This is NOT radical obedience to Christ, this is works done out of the flesh (to feel good about ourselves, to earn our way to God's good graces, or for recognition and acknowledgement). As believers, we must safeguard the distinctness of God's saving work over and against our own efforts. Christians, primary concern should be for the "outflow of the gospel." This means "putting everything in our lives on the table before God" and being "*willing* to sacrifice good things in the church in order to experience the greater things of God."

Choosing Love Over Fear

> "He who does not love has not become acquainted with God [does not and never did know Him], for God is love... There is no fear in love [dread does not exist], but full-grown (complete, perfect) love turns fear out of doors *and* expels every trace of terror! For fear brings with it the thought of punishment, and [so] he who is afraid has not reached the full maturity of love [is not yet grown into love's complete perfection]. (1 John 4:8,18, AMP)

John points out that he who fears does so because he is immature in love. Often this type of immaturity anticipates pain, torture, or punishment. "Fear" in the Greek language is the word *phobeomai* which means "to be frightened", "alarmed", or "terrified". Yet John argued that the person who stands in a relationship of love with God need not be afraid of love. If a person is afraid of love, he or she does not yet have a mature relationship with God. As the love of God matures in every believer, fear begins to dissipate.

So how do we express the love of God to others? Do we love from a heart of purity? Or do we love with selfish motives and ambitions, revealing our fears? The purity of heart can be tested when we pour our Christ-like love into someone that is incapable of offering anything in return (James 1:27).

Beloved, do you let fear of rejection hinder your love for others? Do you allow yourself to be authentic and vulnerable with friends or loved ones? What about your love for God? Do you fear if you love God wholeheartedly He may ask you to do something radical or give up something in return?

Often we cannot see the magnificent gifts that are in store for us because fear scews our vision for the future. Our attitude should be "sink or swim,

I'm going to trust God and give it all I got!" Allow your love for God to mature and override your fears... trusting Him every step of the way.

All that the cross has done for us, we should carry out to others. The cross is a symbol of hope, redemption, restoration, forgiveness, healing, and above all... love.

It is time that believers stop allowing fear to hinder what God has predestined and purposed for every individual. It is time to pick up our swords (the Word of God) and remind ourselves of the resurrection power that indwells within us. There are people in our sphere of influence that need to see the love of Jesus poured out with no reservations of fear. Believers should not respond to fear because before the foundations of the Earth, we were chosen by a perfect-loving God.

Why We Need the Holy Spirit

"And I will ask the Father, and He will give you another Comforter (Counselor, Helper, Intercessor, Advocate, Strengthener, and Standby), that He may remain with you forever— The Spirit of Truth, Whom the world cannot receive (welcome, take to its heart), because it does not see Him or know *and* recognize Him. But you know *and* recognize Him, for He lives with you [constantly] and will be in you. I will not leave you as orphans [comfortless, desolate, bereaved, forlorn, helpless]; I will come [back] to you." (John 14:16-18, AMP)

It's such a beautiful story of God's love for us. When Jesus left this Earth, He did not leave us abandoned as orphans but sent another Helper and Comforter. So why *do* we need this "Comforter" in our lives if we have the Holy Bible?

The Holy Spirit is a mediator and an intercessor that dwells in every believer and serves as the revealer of God's Word, His Will, is a Teacher, Comforter, and Counselor. In addition, the Holy Spirit "illuminates" and shines light and understanding on the Word of God. Without it, we are liable to pluck out our eyeballs and cut off our hands in accordance to Matthew 5:29-30. Now, did God *really* want us to pluck out our eyeballs and cut off our hands as the Word says? Of course not! Through the Holy Spirit we are able to understand that God was revealing the severity of sin. Without revelation through the Holy Spirit, there would be a lot of people walking around with missing body parts!

"Holy Spirit" in the original language is *ruach* which means "wind" or "breath". When we became a believer, God breathed His breathe of life into us and gave us His Holy Spirit. The *instant* we receive Jesus Christ as Lord and Savior, there He is, the Comforter and Helper to guide us and lead us in every decision making process of our lives. It is because of His Holy Spirit that we can know God deeply and intimately.

The Holy Spirit is essential in order to understand God, His Word, and guidance while living in a sinful world. The Holy Spirit gives every believer "advice" while living the Christian life. Although the Bible reveals the character of God and is essential for everyday living, the Holy Spirit guides each individual personally while making personal decisions such as who to marry, what job to take, what church to attend, and answer many other questions that one may have in their life.

The Bible presents the role of the Holy Spirit as a continuation of the work of God in the life of every believer. As such He is an essential companion of every Christian and is the guarantee and means until we reach the pearly gates of Heaven.

Walking in a Spirit of Excellence

"It pleased [King] Darius [successor to Belshazzar] to set over the kingdom 120 satraps who should be [in charge] throughout all the kingdom, And over them three presidents—of whom Daniel was one—that these satraps might give account to them and that the king should have no loss *or* damage. Then this Daniel was distinguished above the presidents and the satraps because an excellent spirit was in him, and the king thought to set him over the whole realm." (Daniel 6:1-3, AMP)

Daniel was recognized by the king and stood out above all the rest because he did everything with a spirit of excellence. To walk in a spirit of excellence is to go above and beyond what is required of you. Walking in a spirit of excellence does not come naturally, however, believers can excel in all we do through the power of God. Without God, we can be ordinary, boring, timid, insecure, and unimpressive, but *with* God, we can walk in divine power and recognize His Spirit at work.

Most often what one exudes outwardly, depicts their inward worth. Individuals who don't know their true value in Christ will tackle tasks "halfway". How they feel about themselves is evident in how they keep their home, their yards, or themselves. But someone who walks in a spirit if excellence will tend to even the small things. God says that a man or woman who is "faithful in little will be entrusted with much" (Luke 16:10).

Do all things as you are doing them unto Jesus. Got housework to do? Do it as unto Jesus. Got a job to do? Do it as unto Jesus. Got a ministry to do? Do it as unto Jesus. Got children to raise? Do it as unto Jesus.

As Christians we are in a unique position to change our homes, our workplace, and our society. The world is watching how we conduct ourselves. It is vital that we recognize that we represent Christ and this includes living a life that is beyond "mediocre". This "middle-of-the-road" servant hood does not properly portray the God we serve. Whatever we do we must do it unto the Lord and we should draw many *towards* the cross, not away from it. Our walk with God should inspire people to evaluate their own lives and path with God.

We should always ascertain to walk in a spirit of excellence because we represent Christ. God has given us the mandate, to walk in the spirit of excellence.

Godly living should rise above the mediocre "barely getting by" standards of the world. Today I encourage you with all that you do, give it all you got and walk in a spirit of excellence.

THE GIFT OF FORGIVENESS

> "Judge not [neither pronouncing judgment nor subjecting to censure], and you will not be judged; do not condemn *and* pronounce guilty, and you will not be condemned *and* pronounced guilty; acquit *and* forgive *and* release (give up resentment, let it drop), and you will be acquitted *and* forgiven *and* released. Give, and [gifts] will be given to you; good measure, pressed down, shaken together, and running over, will they pour into [the pouch formed by] the bosom [of your robe and used as a bag]. For with the measure you deal out [with the measure you use when you confer benefits on others], it will be measured back to you." (Luke 6:37-38, AMP)

Quite often it is easy to give of our time, money, and talents. But how easy is it to give a gift of undeserved forgiveness?

Interestingly, the Book of Luke urges us to "give" right AFTER he tells us to "forgive".

"To give" in the original language is **doron** which means an "expression of honor" and "of a spiritual or supernatural gift" (John 4:20, Acts 8:20, Acts 11:17). In the New Testament, gifts were often given "for the support of the temple and the needs of the poor" (Matt 15:5, Mark 7:11, Luke 21:1).

Today we don't have "temples" per say. However, each individual in which God dwells *is* His temple. So now we can honor God by giving the gift of forgiveness in support of His temple *(God's people)* and the poor *(in spirit)*. Imagine yourself giving an offering to God as you give the gift of forgiveness to the person that needs to be forgiven. Seeing it from this perspective can free them and you!

It is a supernatural gift because every part of our fleshy being does NOT want to forgive where there has been offense, hurt, or wrongdoing. When we forgive, it is a supernatural act of the spirit of God giving an offering to God himself!

Forgiveness is not a gift you give to another person. Forgiveness is not necessarily a gift you give to yourself (although this has been taught in a lot of well-meaning Christian circles, it is done with a selfish and impure motive). Forgiveness is a gift we give to God. No wonder He says He will give back to us in "good measure".

This is how Christians make *real* forgiveness an ongoing, practical part of everyday life, not just a popular spiritual catchword. To recognize that it is a gift to GOD.

So when you forgive someone beloved. Don't look at it as you are doing THEM a favor, but realize that you are offering a supernatural gift to the Spirit of God.

ASSUMPTIONS OF THE ACCUSER

"Stop and think! Do the innocent die? When
have the upright been destroyed?
My experience shows that those who plant trouble and
cultivate evil will harvest the same. A breath from God
destroys them. They vanish in a blast of his anger."
(Job 4:7-9, NLT)
(Eliphaz Assuming Job has Sinned)

"And if you are pure and live with integrity, he will
surely rise up and restore your happy home."
(Job 8:6, NLT)
(Bildad Assuming Job Needs to Repent)

"Should I remain silent while you babble on? When you
mock God, shouldn't someone make you ashamed?
You claim, 'My beliefs are pure,' and 'I am clean in the sight of God.'
If only God would speak; if only he would tell you what he thinks!"
(Job 11:3-5, NLT)
(Zophar Assuming Job is Guilty of Wrongdoing)

"Are you still trying to maintain your integrity? Curse God and die."
(Job 2:9, NLT)
(Job's Wife Assuming Suffering is God's Fault)

Job's wife has harshly been called "the helpmate of the devil". However, it may not be too far from the truth. Anytime accusations or wrong assumptions have been made, it is safe to say that the Enemy is at work. God deals with us through the conviction of the Holy Spirit and through the TRUTH of the Word of God, not through others' false assumptions and accusations.

Eliphaz argued that God punishes the wicked and rewards the righteous. However, his argument was not based on God's truth, but on his own personal experiences. Therefore, he assumed that sin must be at the root of Job's suffering.

Zophar's and Bildad's argument for repentance had some truth, however, they were wrong about Job's reason for suffering.

Job's friends even accused God and assumed that "the hand of The Lord has done this". Their motive, was caused by pure speculation on their part which created even more anguish for Job (talk about "adding salt to the wound")!

When confusion and disappointment are intertwined, it can rapidly lead to impaired judgment, wrong assumptions, and accusations. One must be extremely careful when *responding* and *receiving* from someone who gives bitter advice that comes from an immature faith.

The truth of the matter is that Satan was the first accuser. He went to God accusing Job and assuming that if everything was stripped from him, he would no longer be faithful to God (Job 1:6-12). Shortly after we can see all the wrong assumptions made by the people closest to him.

In the end, The Lord vindicated Job and made him more prosperous than ever before.

As people of God, let us not accept something as true without having the facts or valid proof. Satan sought out to believe the worst in people. If we must assume anything, let us assume the best in people.

Refraining from Lying Lips

"Too much talk leads to sin. Be sensible and keep your mouth shut."
(Proverbs 10:19, NLT)

The above scripture is quite poignant. Lying lips can kill the spirit of unity in the workplace, home, and church. Whereas, a spirit of unity can effectively produce power, agreement, harmony, and God's presence. Any action or practice of deceiving someone by concealing or misrepresenting the truth is sin.

The tongue is often used as a powerful weapon intended to destroy. Often when people gossip about others, it is because they are jealous, vindictive, angry, hateful, grudgeful, or defiant. When we speak ill will of another individual, we are not only harming *them*, but we are harming ourselves. When we deceive with our mouths, we are walking in agreement with Satan because he is the one who deceives and slanders. The Bible is filled with scriptures that warn against speaking negatively about others. Here are a few:

"The wives of elders and deacons must not be slanderers." (1 Timothy 3:11)

"Backbiters are worthy of death and so are people who approve of others who practice it." (Romans 1:30,32)

"Revilers in a local church should be withdrawn from (if they don't repent)." (1 Corinthians 5:11)

Godly attributes are personified in one who refrains from gossiping about others and is dignified, noble, warm, and caring. In the long run, this type of character will bring a satisfying life. Speaking deceit about another can feel satisfying for a moment, but speaking deceit to fulfill instant self-gratification will ultimately bring the gossiper to ruin (Ouch! That's challenging!).

We all have exaggerated, gossiped and lied (albeit a little "white lie") at one time or another. However keep in mind, that we are all held accountable to The Lord for what comes out of our mouths. I believe it *grieves* the heart of God to see His children speaking negatively of one another. I wonder what would happen if we began to see the best in people and spoke THAT into their lives to build them up instead of speaking negatively into their lives to break them down? I am sure the end result would be one of God's miraculous manifested presence. Let the words spoken from your lips lead to life. Those that follow behind you, will learn and be blessed.

A Heart of Deception

"But a certain man named Ananias with his wife Sapphira sold a piece of property, and with his wife's knowledge *and* connivance he kept back *and* wrongfully appropriated some of the proceeds, bringing only a part and putting it at the feet of the apostles. But Peter said, 'Ananias, why has Satan filled your heart that you should lie to *and* attempt to deceive the Holy Spirit, and should [in violation of your promise] withdraw secretly *and* appropriate to your own use part of the price from the sale of the land? Why then, is it that you have proposed *and* purposed in your heart to do this thing? [How could you have the heart to do such a deed?] You have not [simply] lied to men [playing false and showing yourself utterly deceitful] but to God.'

Upon hearing these words, Ananias fell down and died. And great dread *and* terror took possession of all who heard of it. Now after an interval of about three hours his wife came in, not having learned of what had happened. Then Peter said to her, 'How could you two have agreed *and* conspired together to try to deceive the Spirit of the Lord? Listen! The feet of those who have buried your husband are at the door, and they will carry you out [also].' And instantly she fell down at his feet and died; and the young men entering found her dead, and they carried her out and buried her beside her husband. And the whole church and all others who heard of these things were appalled [great awe and strange terror and dread seized them]." (Acts 5:1-11, AMP)

The story of Ananias and Sapphira reveals that even the early church consisted of imperfect people. This couple purposed in their hearts to withhold money that should have been given to the congregation. The end result of their deception led to both of their deaths.

Honesty and deceit cannot remain within the same body. If there is any deceit in an individual or a church body, it will always override the decision to act upon an upright heart of God.

A heart of deception always leads to more deception. However, as in the case of Ananias and Sapphira, soon enough the deceiver will be found and revealed. Before long, the individual is caught in such a web of lies that it is difficult to climb back out. When deception is exposed, it will be like a "death" to him or her who has lived a life of deception because the enemy can no longer be used through the deceiver. It is only through having a relationship with Christ that the individual living a fraudulent life can relearn how to live a life of sincerity and truthfulness.

The spirit of deception still thrives in individuals (and in churches) today. The threat of it should alarm every individual and congregation. God does not allow deception and dishonesty to continue in His relationship with His people. If allowed to remain, the heart will begin to harden… our view of God blurred…and His voice skewed.

NOT FORSAKEN

"Never! Can a mother forget her nursing child? Can she feel no love for the child she has borne? But even if that were possible, I would not forget you! See, I have written your name on the palms of my hands. Always in my mind is a picture of Jerusalem's walls in ruins." (Isaiah 49:15-16, NLT)

Nothing can separate us from the love of Christ. Neither death nor life, neither angels nor demons, neither our fears for today nor our worries about tomorrow—not even the powers of hell can separate us from God's love. No power in the sky above or in the earth below—indeed, nothing in all creation will ever be able to separate us from the love of God that is revealed in Christ Jesus our Lord (Romans 8:38-39).

Even the sorrow of our hearts cannot separate us from Him. Whenever one starts to doubt, feel anxious, fearful, or nervous, remember that there is a God that desires to sooth every ache of your soul. God can cause the unique circumstances of your life to bear fruit. Jesus can replace the ashes, mourning, grief, turmoil, and a spirit of heaviness with a spirit of victory, beauty, joy, and praise. Jesus' salvation alone can reverse the curse of misfortune that threatens to overcome His people.

Most of mankind's misery stems from feeling unloved or abandoned. The enemy of this World would like nothing more than to plant seeds of doubt in our minds to make us feel abandoned by God. In the midst of difficult circumstances, it is easy to feel unloved and forsaken. This feeling of abandonment can often feel worse than the direct attacks of the enemy. Even Jesus had felt forsaken by God, crying out from the cross, *"Eli Eli lama sabachthani?"* which is *"My God, my God, why have you forsaken me?"* (Matthew 27:46) However, don't you know beloved that Jesus is now sitting at the right hand of the Father? Fear, oppression, depression not even death could hold HIM down! He is walking in authority and victory and if you are His today, you can wear the victor's crown too!

No matter the turmoil of life albeit in loss that includes relationships, security, marriage, home, job, health, or finances, believers must remember that God has not forsaken us and the turmoils of this life will not last forever. His presence watches over us and He has engraved you and I on the palm of HIS hands.

A Culture Enticed by Sexual Impurity

> "Don't you realize that those who do wrong will not inherit the Kingdom of God? Don't fool yourselves. Those who indulge in sexual sin, or who worship idols, or commit adultery, or are male prostitutes, or practice homosexuality, or are thieves, or greedy people, or drunkards, or are abusive, or cheat people—none of these will inherit the Kingdom of God. Some of you were once like that. But you were cleansed; you were made holy; you were made right with God by calling on the name of the Lord Jesus Christ and by the Spirit of our God." (1 Corinthians 6:9-11, NLT)

Not too long ago, a talk show aired a segment about the film industry shifting away from G-rated movies because "they don't make enough money…and money talks." A movie expert further explained that, "Our culture has become more tolerant of more explicit themes, language, story lines, etc."

The life of a Christian who desires to remain sexually pure can be a constant battleground in a society that has become more tolerant of sexual sin. Nonetheless, for the Christian that stands firm in their biblical beliefs and the disciplines of longing, loneliness, hope, trust, and an unfailing commitment to Christ can be of immeasurable value. A believer who is unable to remain sexually pure while single and committed to Christ, will likely be unable to remain sexually pure when married and committed to a spouse.

Sex outside the confines of marriage proves to lead to polluted, corrupt, infectious, and self-destructive behaviors. To remain pure is to be free from any contamination that would seek to defile an individual's mind, body, or spirit.

The truth is, apart from having a relationship with Christ, no one can remain sexually pure. The lusts of the flesh are much more enticing than the strength it takes to remain pure. However, when one has a relationship with Christ, we are able to experience a pure and holy God. Thus, exposing the dark hidden secrets of sin and magnifying the beauty of purity. It is until that point that the desire to sin lessens and the desire to remain pure becomes more attractive.

Today, mainstream culture has depicted those who have abstained from sexual immorality as being "abnormal". Several years ago, this would not have been the case. In fact, it would have been "abnormal" to find unwed couples being sexually active, a spouse committing adultery, or technology being used to fulfill explicit desires.

All in all, scripture is clear about what God *condones* and what He *condemns* when it comes to sex. The enemy of this world has used every tool to pervert what God intended to be beautiful within the confines of marriage. Human beings are much more than just sexual figures, we are created in the image of a magnificent, holy, and pure God that desires to be present in every area of our lives.

The Silent Killer

"We don't enjoy being disciplined. It always seems to cause more pain than joy. But later on, those who learn from that discipline have peace that comes from doing what is right. Strengthen your tired arms and weak knees. Keep walking along straight paths so that your injured leg won't get worse. Instead, let it heal. Try to live peacefully with everyone, and try to live holy lives, because if you don't, you will not see the Lord. Make sure that everyone has kindness from God so that bitterness doesn't take root and grow up to cause trouble that corrupts many of you." (Hebrews 12:11-15, GW)

Every believer experiences heartache, disappointment, and difficulties in their lifetime. God does not bestow suffering for sufferings sake nor does (contrary to popular belief) suffering make a person stronger. It is how the individual *responds* to that suffering that makes them stronger.

God is faithful in providing His grace even through the turbulent times. It is through the sufferings that often bring a believer to a bended knee, seeking the ONE that knows all. Seeking the ONE that knows the beginning from the end. He provides His loving grace to soothe the wound in times of hurting.

However, it is not the trials in and of themselves that cause a Christian to feel pain. It is another "silent killer" that overtakes the mind, will, emotions, and then eventually...the heart. It creeps in marriages, friendships, relationships, and churches - seemingly unnoticed until it is too late. At first, it isn't obvious to the onlooker. It sneaks in silently until it has overtaken its victim. This "silent killer" is the deadly sting of BITTERNESS. The deadly effects of bitterness are wide-ranging... impacting everyone, even if from afar.

So how does one guard themselves against becoming a victim from this deadly "disease"? The key is FORGIVENESS. Every believer has the opportunity to either forgive or dwell upon the wrong they feel they have incurred. Opportunities to receive the sting of bitterness will surely come. One can know how to truly forgive when they have first turned to Christ and have experienced forgiveness in their own lives. The greatest character revealed in Christians is when a Christian is able to replace bitterness with love and forgive those who have greatly wronged them.

Beloved, if you are experiencing bitterness in your heart today, I encourage you to cling to faith and walk in forgiveness and love. These steps are vital in order to conquer overwhelming adversity and move forward into God's purpose for your future. Allow God to cleanse your heart and restore you to a right relationship with Him and with others. Once you do so, you will experience joy again and see beyond your circumstances and into God's plan for your life.

God's Justice

> "The Lord saw that the wickedness of man was great in
> the earth, and that every imagination *and* intention of
> all human thinking was only evil continually.
> And the Lord regretted that He had made man on the earth, and
> He was *grieved* at heart. So the Lord said, I will destroy, blot out,
> *and* wipe away mankind, whom I have created from the face of
> the ground—not only man, [but] the beasts and the creeping
> things and the birds of the air—for it grieves Me *and* makes
> Me regretful that I have made them." (Genesis 6:5-7, AMP)

It saddens me to think there are times where the Lord is regretful of having made mankind. It is not that our God doesn't love us, however, the wickedness of man and the harm that is inflicted on ourselves and others causes God's heart to be remorseful.

Our minds cannot begin to grasp why God would destroy a town, a land, or a city. Two main reasons exist for His command:

1) The inhabitants of the land had turned themselves over to wickedness and depravity
2) If the innocent would continue to coexist with these wicked people, they would either be *infected* or *affected* by them

When God said He would *"wipe away mankind"*, this included *all* mankind - not just the guilty. The innocent had to be *"wiped away"* as well.

Though the loss of innocent life is devastating, it can lead to hearts that are radically abandoned towards God, moving radically in the Christian faith, and ultimately saving a community.

Today believers live in the most perverse and depraved generation in all of history. Our secular world worships the same wickedness (and even more so) than the biblical pagan predecessors before our time.

The goddess of Asherah is noted for war and murder.

The god of Molech is noted for killing innocent babes.

Jezebel is noted for luring men into sexual impurity.

Sodom and Gomorrah was destroyed for approving homosexuality.

Much like today, they did *everything* that God hated. These people had known God and because of *HIS* mercy and grace, He had given them ample time to turn from their wicked ways. No doubt that mankind's actions *grieves* the heart of God. He sees the pain, the heartache, and the injustice. And though He is patient and merciful, He is a just and righteous God. He does what is right. He will judge the sin. He will judge mankind. He will judge the land. All of Heaven and Earth will await to see the final outcome of HIS Judgment Day.

Freedom From Addiction

✠

"In [this] freedom Christ has made us free [and completely liberated us]; stand fast then, and do not be hampered and held ensnared and submit again to a yoke of slavery [which you have once put off]". (Galatians 5:1, AMP)

In this scripture, Paul once again, encouraged the people of Galatia to stand firm in their faith and not return to a life of bondage. Christ died to set us free and through the power of His resurrection, we can experience great freedom in every area of our lives. Simply "stopping" an addiction or a certain bondage will not bring true healing in a person's life. It is important to get to the root cause of the addiction. The addiction itself is just a "mask" to cover up the inter turmoil of experiencing feelings such as pain, shame, guilt, dissatisfaction and disappointment of having unmet needs. These underlying feelings and pain must be healed in order to experience true freedom from bondage... the type of freedom that only Christ can bring. Simply removing the "mask" (or addiction) only leads to further turmoil and an increased risk to return to the addiction or substitute for another one.

Healing begins when a person recognizes that an addiction exists and acknowledges that he or she is unable to overcome the addiction with their own power. Many people have experienced freedom from alcohol by acknowledging the FIRST step in Alcoholics Anonymous, "We admit we are powerless over our addiction..." And step THREE, "We make the decision to turn our will and lives over to the care of God..." Just reading this can bring much freedom! Although these are just a couple of steps mentioned in the AA program, they are key confessions that can be applied to *any* area of bondage.

To experience healing and freedom, there must be a willingness to allow God to touch and meet the underlying need. As God begins to heal the deeper need, the addict will find themselves being led by the Spirit instead of being led by the addiction.

> "In Christ there is freedom from bondage. Believers are no longer slaves; they are free-not through their own merit but through God's redeeming grace." - Rhonda H. Kelley

FIGHTING WELL

"He was despised and rejected *and* forsaken by men, a Man of sorrows *and* pains, and acquainted with grief *and* sickness; and like One from Whom men hide their faces He was despised, and we did not appreciate His worth *or* have any esteem for Him. Surely He has borne our griefs (sicknesses, weaknesses, and distresses) and carried our sorrows *and* pains [of punishment], yet we [ignorantly] considered Him stricken, smitten, and afflicted by God [as if with leprosy]. But He was wounded for our transgressions, He was bruised for our guilt *and* iniquities; the chastisement [needful to obtain] peace *and* well-being for us was upon Him, and with the stripes [that wounded] Him we are healed *and* made whole. (Isaiah 53:3-5, AMP)

There has never been anyone that has incurred greater wounds than that of Jesus. He was betrayed by friends, forgotten by parents, accused my many, rejected by others, and despised by almost everyone.

Yet still, Jesus fought well. It takes a great strength to have been oppressed and afflicted and "open not your mouth". (Isaiah 53:7)

Scripture tell us "yet it pleased The Lord to bruise Him" (v. 10). Our feeble minds cannot begin to comprehend *why* it pleased The Lord to cause pain and affliction. For a brief second one might be fooled into thinking that the character of God is one of tyranny. But that is not so beloved. The reason that it *"pleased"* Him was because of His immeasurable love for you and for me. When Jesus was being betrayed, it was God inflicting the pain of betrayal upon Himself. When He was forgotten, God was experiencing the pain of being forgotten on Himself. When He was rejected, God was experiencing the pain of rejection on Himself. When He was despised, God was experiencing the pain of being despised by all. And when He was bruised, it was God inflicting pain on Himself. All for you, and for me.

Verse 12 tells us that Jesus "poured out His soul unto death". The soul involves the mind, will, and emotions. Jesus died not only a physical death but He "died" to His own thoughts, His own desires, and His own emotions too. Jesus overcame and in the end, gained the victory. If we have Jesus in our hearts today, we can "die" to our mind, will, and emotions and have the victory too!

Jesus suffered not because He did anything wrong, but because He did everything right. "Sometimes you face difficulties not because you're doing something wrong, but because you're doing everything right!"

Today I encourage you to "fight well". No matter what you are going through "open not your mouth". Jesus incurred much pain but in the end, He got the victory so you and I can have that same victory too!

Stewarding Spiritual Gifts

"As each of you has received a gift (a particular spiritual talent, a gracious divine endowment), employ it for one another as [befits] good trustees of God's many-sided grace [faithful stewards of the extremely diverse powers and gifts granted to Christians by unmerited favor]. Whoever speaks, [let him do it as one who utters] oracles of God; whoever renders service, [let him do it] as with the strength which God furnishes abundantly, so that in all things God may be glorified through Jesus Christ (the Messiah). To Him be the glory and dominion forever and ever (through endless ages). Amen (so be it)." (1 Peter 4:10-11, AMP)

Quite often in church, it can be easy to get caught up in who has what spiritual giftings. In fact, some giftings can create dissension when coveted by others. It is a fleshly characteristic that mankind has wrestled with since the beginning of time (wanting what someone else has or what they *can't* have). However, notice the scripture points out that services must be rendered with "the strength that GOD furnishes". The New King James Version says, "If anyone ministers, let him do it as with the ability which God supplies that in all things God may be glorified..."

Too often Christians want to believe that the spiritual giftings have somehow been EARNED through special sacrifice. However, it is evident through scripture that God Himself supplies the abilities that HE may be glorified. It cannot be earned and to think so gives one a sense of false entitlement. Rest assured, "apart from Him we can do nothing" (John 15:5). God chooses the spiritual giftings to *whom* and *when* He wants to supply them. That's God's business, not ours. To covet, complain, or mishandle giftings is to come against the Almighty Himself, the Gifter of all things, not the vessel in which the giftings are manifested through.

God will require an accounting of each person's stewardship in how they handled their gifts. Christians can be prepared for that day of accountability by taking their stewardship seriously and responsibly. Whatever actions or decisions are made, it must all be pleasing to God.

Talents should be used to build up others and to glorify God. Being good stewards of spiritual gifts comes with the revelation of knowing our personal accountability to God and in doing so, we will do an excellent job of stewarding our spiritual gifts.

Reconciliation

> "And he shall turn *and* reconcile the hearts of the [estranged] fathers to the [ungodly] children, and the hearts of the [rebellious] children to [the piety of] their fathers [a reconciliation produced by repentance of the ungodly], lest I come and smite the land with a curse *and* a ban of utter destruction."
> (Malachi 4:6, Amplified)

There is a devastating threat scouring the earth. It is the threat of dividing families and breaking lives. Nonetheless, we must cling to the promise in the above scripture. Conflicts are almost inevitable in families, but God will not allow situations in families to remain "undone". Reconciliation in families will happen once again.

Reconciliation entails the restoration of trust in a relationship that has been damaged. Both parties must be involved and agreeable to come to a resolution. One or both parties involved in a conflict must set aside the issue or episode and move forward to deliberately taking steps to reconciliation. However, it is important to address and reconcile *old* hurts as both parties may feel as they are "walking on egg shells" and it will take very little effort to create greater risk for future conflict.

2 Corinthians 5:17-21 says, *"Therefore, if anyone is in Christ, the new creation has come: The old has gone, the new is here! All this is from God, who reconciled us to himself through Christ and gave us the ministry of reconciliation: that God was reconciling the world to himself in Christ, not counting people's sins against them. And he has committed to us the message of reconciliation. We are therefore Christ's ambassadors, as though God were making his appeal through us. We implore you on Christ's behalf: Be reconciled to God. God made him who had no sin to be sin for us, so that in him we might become the righteousness of God."*

Beloved, do you know what that means? That means that because Christ has reconciled Himself to us, we too can know and experience reconciliation with loved ones. There is no room for shame, guilt, disappointments, pass regrets, unforgiveness, bitterness, hate, and anger for the one that has been reconciled!

God can bring reconciliation not only with Him, but also in relationships that have once been broken. Fruitful relationships can thrive, not necessarily because the other party has changed, but because *we* as believers have changed. We are a new creation through Christ.

Maybe there are some moms, dads, brothers, sisters, aunts or uncles out there who haven't always done things right. The good news is that radical change occurs when one has a genuine encounter with the Lord Jesus Christ. When we are reconciled to Christ, there is a new way of knowing, a new way of thinking, and a new way of living. In Him, we are a new creation and He alone can bring true restoration, reconciliation, emotional cleansing and healing in families.

Flattering Titles

> "Let me not, I pray you, respect any man's person; Neither will I give flattering titles unto any man. For I know not to give flattering titles; Else would my Maker soon take me away."
> (Job 32: 21-22, ASV)

Elihu feared in giving Job his opinion because he (as well as Job's three companions) were older than he was. In fact, he wasn't going to speak at all because he was convinced that the age of the other three men would teach wisdom. Yet still, using greater wisdom than his predecessors, he waited for the Spirit of God to reveal to him when the appropriate time to speak would be. He felt the Spirit of the Almighty give *him* the understanding that "great men are not always wise, nor do the aged always understand justice" (Job 32: 6-9). The Spirit of God compelled the youngest man of the group to speak words of wisdom.

Elihu spoke words like a court judge, with justice and without showing partiality. He wanted to be fair to everyone. In doing so, he realized his own purpose. He did not feel the need to lie to try to prove his ideas or to flatter those with great titles to propel his own ambitions. (Quite often it is the individual that is willing to flatter a man due to his title that is willing to quickly abandon that same man when his title is stripped). Elihu's words would be genuine. He was not disrespectful, but spoke truth with sincerity. He knew that God was listening to his words and would one day be held accountable for them. He also knew that God was not only Job's judge, He was Elihu's judge too.

Titles are supposed to be used to bring "order". However, titles quite often convince the "title holder" that they deserve higher acknowledgment than they truly deserve. It is by God's grace alone that the average "layman" would step aside and let someone lead. I have seen men with NO title carrying great authority given by God. And I have also seen men with GREAT titles carrying very little authority when given by man.

In the same token, God is the God of order, not of confusion. Although we must recognize the order of things when certain titles are given, we are not be deterred by them. Especially when the One with the highest authority is speaking to us. Believers have one of the greatest gifts God has given, that is the ability to hear Him speak to us for ourselves, through the precious Holy Spirit. God "is no respecter of persons" (Acts 10:34). He doesn't view any one person "greater" than the next. The more we consider the majesty of God (and not in and of ourselves), the more we are propelled to walking in humility while doing whatever it is He has called us to do. It is wise to respect authority but it is unwise to treat any man with partiality. Do not be easily influenced by rank, age, wealth, or personal friendship. State the truth impartially as Elihu did, and it will deliver you into walking into a whole new level of freedom.

HEALING SHAME

"Therefore, if anyone is in Christ, the new creation has come: The old has gone, the new is here! All this is from God, who reconciled us to himself through Christ and gave us the ministry of reconciliation: that God was reconciling the world to himself in Christ, not counting people's sins against them. And he has committed to us the message of reconciliation. We are therefore Christ's ambassadors, as though God were making his appeal through us. We implore you on Christ's behalf: Be reconciled to God. God made him who had no sin to be sin for us, so that in him we might become the righteousness of God." (2 Corinthians 5:17-21, NIV)

Shame is an emotion that can overtake an individual. Thoughts of "you are a bad person", "you don't deserve to live", and "you are worthless" can often consume someone who is battling the emotion of shame.

When such thoughts are relentless in one's mind, a person can begin to believe the lies and conclude that they deserve a bad life, whether self-imposed or mistreatment by others. This often becomes one's core identity and the result is self-destructing, repetitively making poor decisions and ultimately, obliterating one's hope for the future.

When an individual believes the barrage of lies about themselves, healing must first begin by confessing and then *replacing* those lies with God's biblical truths.

You ARE worthy. (Psalm 139: 13-15)

You DO have a hope and a future. (Jeremiah 29:11)

You ARE loved. (Colossians 3:12-14)

Radical change occurs when one has a genuine encounter with the Lord Jesus Christ. In Christ there is a new way of knowing, a new way of thinking, and a new way of living. In doing so, you will be a new creation and have a new nature that is given through Christ (2 Corinthians 1:12).

Renewed Strength

"Why would you ever complain, O Jacob, or, whine, Israel, saying, "God has lost track of me. He doesn't care what happens to me"? Don't you know anything? Haven't you been listening? God doesn't come and go. God *lasts*. He's Creator of all you can see or imagine. He doesn't get tired out, doesn't pause to catch his breath. And he knows *everything*, inside and out. He energizes those who get tired, gives fresh strength to dropouts. For even young people tire and drop out, young folk in their prime stumble and fall. But those who wait upon God get fresh strength. They spread their wings and soar like eagles. They run and don't get tired, they walk and don't lag behind."
(Isaiah 40:27-31, MSG)

Fatigue can be a nuisance for everyone. Nothing makes a person unable to cope with work, family, household chores, and life circumstances more than fatigue. The most difficult times of service can be in the monotonous, grind of everyday life when we feel like we are spinning our wheels.

Being tired all the time can affect your mind, will, and emotions. However, God has promised to satisfy and replenish your weary soul. Scripture offers ways to feel renewed through fatigue and weariness:

- Support from close friends, family, or church members can help handle stress more effectively. Knowing someone is there to "bear up" the load can make difficult circumstances more tolerable (Isaiah 50:4, Galatians 6:2)
- Invest time in yourself for a sense of renewed strength. Renewal of spirit and energy can enhance productivity and creativity (Eccl 5:8)
- Beware of over commitment and always being a "yes" person. You know how much you can handle. Don't let others guilt you into carrying a burden that is not yours to carry. Learn to say, "no" and reprioritize your responsibilities (Heb 12:1, Matt 6:33)

I encourage you to see God for the powerful Creator that He is. He never tires nor grows weary. All human strength lacks and falls short in comparison to the strength we gain from the omniscient, all-powerful God that we serve. The Lord's children can exchange their weakness for God's strength in our daily walk of life.

For the Working Class

"So I became great and excelled more than all who were before me in Jerusalem. Also my wisdom remained with me. Whatever my eyes desired I did not keep from them. I did not withhold my heart from any pleasure, for my heart rejoiced in all my labor; and this was my reward from all my labor. Then I looked on all the works that my hands had done and on the labor in which I had toiled; and indeed all was vanity and grasping for the wind. There was no profit under the sun."
(Ecclesiastes 2:9-11)

An individual who is employed outside the home has many challenges. Knowing how to juggle all of the responsibilities can become an obstacle. One must evaluate their priorities and decision-making process. Although being employed is a necessary part of survival, a working individual must consider the following:

- Careers are usually based on contracts that are temporary, familial relationships are covenants that are eternal. Employers come and go but family and God are with you for the rest of your life.
- A career *should* play a very small part in a person's identity. A man or woman should not be categorized by what they do but in who they are. Who they are is largely demonstrated through their relationship with God.

God's criteria for success is faithfulness. (Regardless of how the "world" or the American "system" defines success). God is so merciful that He honors not only an individual's efforts, but their intentions.

Family members or colleagues may not see the big picture of a Christian's life, but God does.

In addition, a Christian should not be found slandering or gossiping about their employer (see Titus 2:3). However, an employer has no right to ask an employee to lie or deceive in any way. A working man or woman does not owe their employer participation in any activity that is dishonorable. This includes any social occasions marked by lewd conversations and sinful behavior.

While an employee owes their employer an honest day's work, they do not owe all of their time and energy. This leaves a person, at the end of the workday, with nothing to give to their family members when they return home. God created and expects a balanced lifestyle with family, home, and the workplace. Priorities should be firmly established according to His divine order.

Dealing with Emotions

> "I will say to God my Rock, Why have You forgotten me? Why go I mourning because of the oppression of the enemy? As with a sword [crushing] in my bones, my enemies taunt *and* reproach me, while they say continually to me, Where is your God?" (Psalm 42:9-10, AMP) "Judge *and* vindicate me, O God; plead and defend my cause against an ungodly nation. O deliver me from the deceitful and unjust man! For You are the God of my strength [my Stronghold—in Whom I take refuge]; why have You cast me off? Why go I mourning because of the oppression of the enemy?" (Psalm 43:1-2, AMP)

Often we can see an individual's "inward" beliefs by how they express their emotions "outwardly". We are created in God's image (Genesis 1:27), which also includes our mind, will, and emotions. He too is a God of emotions!

He is a God that is *passionate* in His pursuant after His people. He is a God that *grieves* at the rebellion of His children. He is a God that gets *angry* over idolatry but *delights* over having communion with His children. God longs to be able to have a relationship with us even more so than we long to be in communion with Him.

Mankind is made of a mix of mind, will, and emotions that shapes every individual's personality. Some personalities reveal a hardened heart... an emotion that is used to build up a wall of protection. Other personalities reveal a sensitive heart... an emotion that often leads to feelings of brokenness and despair. Although both are common human emotions, neither extreme is as God intended it.

As Christians, we have quite often been taught that to experience or reveal pain, sadness, or anger is to sin. However, to reveal human emotion, whether good or bad, it to feel ALIVE. Dangerously, when emotions are suppressed or denied, it can often lead to a self-destructing lifestyle that hinders God's potential in every believer.

Emotions are a part of our human "make-up" that helps us become relatable with a heart of compassion towards one another. However, most importantly, it helps us relate to God in a much deeper and meaningful way.

Although emotions are part of our genetic make-up, it is important to recognize that they must never rule us. We must submit our emotions to a will that is yielded to God. All emotion must be yielded to God and dealt with in a godly manner so that we will not cause injury, strong arm, or manipulate God's people.

It's A New Season

"For behold, the winter is past,
The rain is over and gone.
The flowers have already appeared in the land;
The time has arrived for pruning the vines,
And the voice of the turtledove has been heard in our land.
The fig tree has ripened its figs,
And the vines in blossom have given forth their fragrance.
Arise, my darling, my beautiful one,
And come along!"
Song of Solomon 2:11-13 (NASB)

God's goodness is nowhere more apparent than in the midst of the long, bitter, cold winter seasons of your life. Those that have God in their lives can stand firm in full confidence knowing that they will overcome as victors (not victims), no matter what cruelties life tries to throw them. Believers are precious in God's sight and He greatly delights in them. Though we may often go through chilling times, God is still with us and we need not fear the dark, cloudy surroundings we sometimes find ourselves in. God promises to do a new thing every season - something that has never been done before, some unheard of and wonderful event, that shall far surpass all that has been formerly done (Isaiah 42:9). This is a great hope!

Just as in nature, when the warmer months of your life comes forth, your eyes will once again be opened to the green grass springing forth, the buds opening with new leaves and flowers while releasing their sweet fragrance. Once again you will see and hear lovely birds burst into song. All beautiful figures of nature revealing God's manner of the *new* that is coming to pass in your life.

Similarly, believers are beautiful to Him as we are clothed in the righteousness of Christ. We are fragrant and a sweet aroma to His nostrils as He graces us with His Spirit. Every believer thrives under the refreshing beams of the Sun of righteousness.

Harsh, bitter seasons can be a barren tree to the soul; but Christ is a fruitful one. When thirsty and weary souls are parched with the troubles of this world, they can rest assured that they will find their deliverance in Christ. Believers have tasted that the Lord Jesus is gracious; his fruits are all the precious privileges of a relationship with Him.

Throughout our lifetime, we will experience many changes and challenges. However, as we enter into a new season of our life, let us move forward with expectation and excitement. Let us open our eyes to new opportunities and leave the past disappointments and failures behind. If you are entering into a change in your life, trust and embrace God every step of the way. Let fresh anointing and restoration come your way. Forget about the bitter cold, harsh, and long winter you've endured. That's all behind you now. Remember that in this change of your life, God is going to do a new thing!

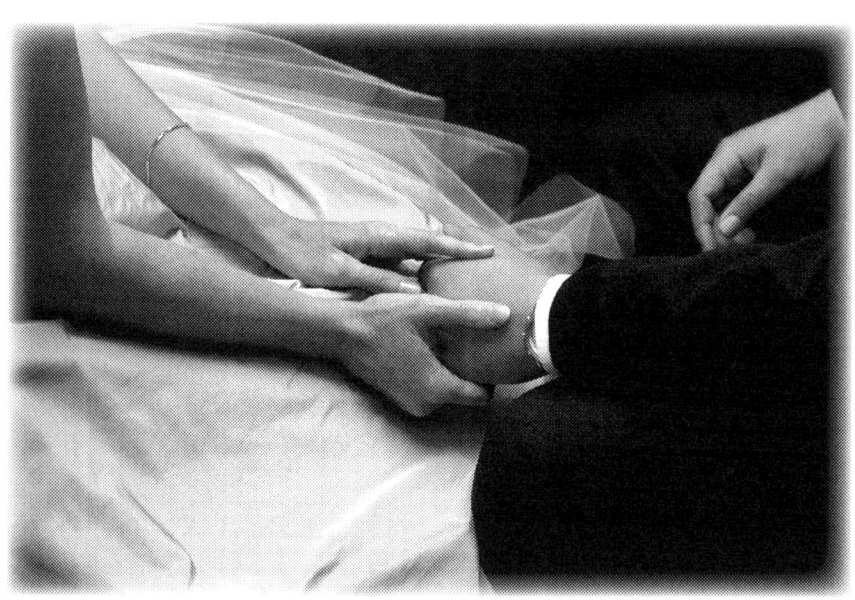

Principles of Marriage

"The Lord God said, 'It is not good for the man to be alone. I will make a helper suitable for him.'" (Genesis 2:18, NIV)

In the oldest marriage covenant of the world, God created Adam to be the provider, the protector, and the leader. It is a direct representation of Jesus' type of servant leadership.

Certainly Jesus did not treat His Bride (the church) with an abusive or tyrannical attitude. Nor should a bride have a willful disregard for her husband's leadership.

The Bible is clear about a woman's responsibilities to her husband. She is to be a helper, a comforter, and an encourager. Eve was to encourage Adam in fulfilling God's purpose. She was a blessing sent from God and was the closest companion he had on earth, relieving his loneliness.

God's principles of marriage remain the same today. He has depicted specific roles for both husband and wife. Husbands are to use their God-given authority to provide, protect, and lead. Wives are to help their husbands become all God has purposed them to be.

Husbands and wives can ignore God's divine order for the household. However, it is important to note that when godly principles are violated, strife and division are ever present.

Today I encourage married couples to find time, energy, and creative ways to conform to God's principles for a fruitful, peaceful, and godly marriage.

THE SAMARITAN WOMAN

"A woman, a Samaritan, came to draw water. Jesus said, 'Would you give me a drink of water?' (His disciples had gone to the village to buy food for lunch.) The Samaritan woman, taken aback, asked, 'How come you, a Jew, are asking me, a Samaritan woman, for a drink?' (Jews in those days wouldn't be caught dead talking to Samaritans.) Jesus answered, 'If you knew the generosity of God and who I am, you would be asking *me* for a drink, and I would give you fresh, living water.'"
(John 4:7-10, MSG)

The Samaritan woman went to the well to draw water at the hottest time of the day. So much was her guilt and shame that she refused to be in the presence of the other townspeople. Yet still, it is during this difficult task that she met Jesus face to face, revealing to her who she really was through revealing himself.

Jesus was not bound by the social rules of His time. He broke the mold by:

1) Speaking to a woman in public (Middle Eastern men were never to speak to a woman in public)
2) Speaking to a *Samaritan* woman (Jews and Samaritan's hated each other as racial tensions increased)
3) Speaking to a woman of such despicable reputation. After all, no self-respecting Jewish teacher would waste their time on such a woman (She was known for having many husbands)

His main purpose on this earth was to "heal the brokenhearted, proclaim liberty to the captives, and open the prison doors to those who are bound" (Isaiah 61)... and so it should be with every believer.

Jesus disregarded the social barriers and offered a new life of forgiveness and redemption.

Once the Samaritan woman had the encounter with Jesus, she drank of the "living water" and left her water pot behind. She had quickly forgotten her guilt and shame and no longer hid from the townspeople but ran *to* them. In spite of everything, *she* was the one that had just had an encounter with the Messiah!

Every believer should take hold of the Jesus that removes all sin, guilt, shame, and condemnation. In doing so, one cannot help but share the good news in every town, city, and State. This is the call, purpose, and destiny of every believer.

> "Therefore go and make disciples of all nations, baptizing them in the name of the Father and of the Son and of the Holy Spirit." (Matthew 28:19, NIV)

A LIFE OF SINGLENESS, NOT LONELINESS

"Now there are distinctive varieties and distributions of endowments (gifts, extraordinary powers distinguishing certain Christians, due to the power of divine grace operating in their souls by the Holy Spirit) and they vary, but the [Holy] Spirit remains the same. And there are distinctive varieties of service and ministration, but it is the same Lord [Who is served]. And there are distinctive varieties of operation [of working to accomplish things], but it is the same God Who inspires and energizes them all in all. But to each one is given the manifestation of the [Holy] Spirit [the evidence, the spiritual illumination of the Spirit] for good and profit. To one is given in and through the [Holy] Spirit [the power to speak] a message of wisdom, and to another [the power to express] a word of knowledge and understanding according to the same [Holy] Spirit; To another [wonder-working] faith by the same [Holy] Spirit, to another the extraordinary powers of healing by the one Spirit; To another the working of miracles, to another prophetic insight (the gift of interpreting the divine will and purpose); to another the ability to discern and distinguish between [the utterances of true] spirits [and false ones], to another various kinds of [unknown] tongues, to another the ability to interpret [such] tongues. All these [gifts, achievements, abilities] are inspired and brought to pass by one and the same [Holy] Spirit, Who apportions to each person individually [exactly] as He chooses." (1 Corinth 12:4-11, AMP)

God has predestined each individual to carry a gift that opens doors for unique opportunities. These prospects, more often than not, are God-given opportunities for the betterment of various members of the body.

During times of singleness or "aloneness", one must not become embittered, feeling forsaken by God. Adam had the most intimate times with Lord in the garden before Eve was created. These times of solitude should be viewed as an honor and a privilege; a response of a great committed faith, not a lonely one.

An individual who is single or alone should harken to the call of having a deep covenant relationship with God, seizing the opportunity to develop their gifts.

Seasons of aloneness is a call to develop a deep love relationship with the Lord. In turn, the individual can overflow in a pure, productive, and generous love that will impact others. This type of spiritual vitality can be used as an anchor and source of stability, it does not need to be viewed as a time of weakness or fragility in one's life.

The person who is experiencing a season of solitude can experience great freedom as they devote themselves to work, friendship, and service - all of which is necessary to further God's kingdom.

A generous willingness to assist others is the key to happiness and fulfillment for the individual who feels alone. Focusing on the needs of others with a generous service is a tremendous witness to the power of God, and one of the greatest gifts that should be sought after from God. In the long run, the heart of servitude is less likely to be consumed by the temptation of self-pity and better yet, more likely to see God's working power through them.

A Fraudulent Faith

> "But what I do, I will continue to do, [for I am determined to maintain this independence] in order to cut off the claim of those who would like [to find an occasion and incentive] to claim that in their boasted [mission] they work on the same terms that we do. For such men are false apostles [spurious, counterfeits], deceitful workmen, masquerading as apostles (special messengers) of Christ (the Messiah). And it is no wonder, for Satan himself masquerades as an angel of light; So it is not surprising if his servants also masquerade as ministers of righteousness. [But] their end will correspond with their deeds." (2 Corinthians 11:12-15, AMP)

It is clear from reading the above passage that Satan has the ability to mask himself as "an angel of light". The false apostles in the church of Corinth were knowingly perverting the truth and were somewhat "cultic" in dealing with others and one another. Outwardly, they appeared to be religious (ministers of righteousness), but they perverted the truth of the Word. They thought they were a "special" group of people and often adopted an outlook of exclusivity within their group.

Quite often when we think of a cult, we think of witches, warlocks, and evil spells. However, a "cult" is *any* religious group where there is veneration for one specific individual, believing that truth can be revealed to them alone.

Cult leaders are always authoritarian. They typically encourage their followers to adopt their legalistic lifestyles and mindsets, convincing their group that they alone know what is best for them.

Many people have suffered confusion and brainwashing during these manipulative tactics, fearful of making a decision without the permission and approval of the authoritarian. If a cultic member decides to "break the mold" and make their own decisions, they may experience grievances such as: extortion, bombardment, shunning, and exploitation.

When following a faith, one must be extremely careful not to entangle themselves in such religious circles. Here are a few warning signs of an organization that may be operating in a "cultic" mindset:

1) system of religious worship, particularly in its religious rites.
2) Veneration of a person. Especially in respects to a body of admirers
3) a group bound together by veneration of the same person
4) Exclusivity or dejection of others who don't belong to their sect

In the minds of many Christian leaders, the increase in cult membership is a direct indication of the church's failure to meet individual's needs with genuine Christ-centered principles. Cultic groups often arise when decisions are influenced by man-centered principles.

Be Confident in Who God has Created You to Be

> "Thank you for making me so wonderfully complex! Your workmanship is marvelous—how well I know it. You watched me as I was being formed in utter seclusion, as I was woven together in the dark of the womb. You saw me before I was born. Every day of my life was recorded in your book. Every moment was laid out before a single day had passed. How precious are your thoughts about me, O God. They cannot be numbered!"
> (Psalm 139:14-17, NLT)

Long ago, before the foundations of the Earth, The Lord weaved and knitted our beings in the most intricate ways. God custom designed every one of us, equipping us for a specific achievement and purpose (Isaiah 43:7; Romans 9:20). We are to praise God for the wonderful way in which He has fashioned our mind, bodies, gifts, talents, and anointings. We are to marvel at His magnificent and unique creation for each individual.

In all my travels, I have had the privilege of experiencing many things. In particular, having insight on how many ministries operate. I have had the honor of partnering with ministries that operate well, and have felt the sting from ministries who are not operating well. However, nothing baffles me more than the conquest from ministry leaders to conform others to be like them. Many mean well but it really is a pompous attitude that would make any of us think that an individual "should operate like me". Maybe that youth pastor is supposed to be loud and boisterous because in an overstimulated generation, that is what gets the youths attention. Maybe it's okay for that woman to be a confident individual in God because that will give her the strength she needs to uplift other women in Christ. Maybe it's okay for that man not to wear a suit, have tattoos and shaggy hair for the people God has called him to reach.

Although it is wise to learn from great predecessors who have gone before us, God has called us to learn from them.... not be like them. The vision often gets skewed, lines blurred, and boundaries crossed when one is given permission to teach another. I emphasis "given permission" because we cannot force our will on others. It is only by permission that one is able to teach, lead, pastor, or mentor. So often people in these types of positions feel it is their right. No beloved, it is your privilege.

Maybe you are someone who is struggling in your abilities today. Maybe you are someone who is being told to change the way you operate in your giftings. Maybe you are confused in your purpose or calling. Maybe you have been shamed for being the person God has created you to be. Today I encourage you... You are the person God has called you to be for the people God has called you to reach.

So be forgiving when well-meaning spiritual authorities try to make you more like them, they know not what they do (Luke 23:34). Respect them, learn from them, but do not alter who God has created you to be for the pleasure of man. Be confident (not arrogant) in who God has made you to be for the pleasure of God.

"Authority does not mean more people to control. Authority means more responsibility to SERVE... more feet to wash." - Dr. Johnathan Welton

Scribes and Pharisees

> "So observe and practice all they tell you; but do not do
> what they do, for they preach, but do not practice.
> They tie up heavy loads, *hard to bear*, and place them on men's
> shoulders, but they themselves will not lift a finger to help bear them.
> They do all their works to be seen of men; for they make wide their
> phylacteries (small cases enclosing certain Scripture passages, worn
> during prayer on the left arm and forehead) and make long their
> fringes [worn by all male Israelites, according to the command].
> And they take pleasure in *and* [thus] love the place of
> honor at feasts and the best seats in the synagogues,
> And to be greeted with honor in the marketplaces
> and to have people call them rabbi."
> (Matthew 23:3-7, AMP)

Phylacteries were leather boxes containing Scripture. They were worn by Jewish men during prayer time on the arm or the forehead. Biblical commands were written on small scrolls and placed in the Old Testament frontlets or New Testament phylacteries. The Pharisees and scribes made these phylacteries "show pieces" and larger than common for all to see. They wanted to appear "holier than thou" so to speak. They enjoyed drawing attention to themselves and their supposed ability to adhere to every law in the Scripture. The religious leaders felt they deserved the best and were overly consumed with "labels" and "titles".

However, Jesus condemned the scribes and Pharisees and called them "hypocrites". He despised the rejection of the kingdom, false teachings, self attempts at purification, and self-righteous attitudes towards God's people. Scripture is evidence of Jesus' strong and pointed language (Matthew 23:13-16). His greatest grievance was that the church leaders were laying heavy burdens on the congregation that they themselves were not willing or able to adhere to. He condemned them for drawing more attention towards themselves than the kingdom of Heaven. Yet still, His heart ached over the situation and He yearned to forgive and heal.

As believers in the kingdom of God, our hearts should ache over situations that make His heart ache and yearn to forgive and heal the hurt that we have caused and the hurt that has been caused by others. We must first look at the sin in our own lives and evaluate our hearts and what it truly means to be a Christian. It is not our job as believers to judge others but to point people to the cross and to the Kingdom of Heaven. For the Lord himself will one day come and rule, reign, and judge every church and every believer that is called a "Christian" by name only.

Saved Lives, Changed Lives

"'When a corrupting spirit is expelled from someone, it drifts along through the desert looking for an oasis, some unsuspecting soul it can bedevil. When it doesn't find anyone, it says, 'I'll go back to my old haunt.' On return, it finds the person swept and dusted, but vacant. It then runs out and rounds up seven other spirits dirtier than itself and they all move in, whooping it up. That person ends up far worse than if he'd never gotten cleaned up in the first place.' While he [Jesus] was saying these things, some woman lifted her voice above the murmur of the crowd: 'Blessed the womb that carried you, and the breasts at which you nursed!' Jesus commented, 'Even more blessed are those who hear God's Word and guard it with their lives!'"
(Luke 11:24-28, MSG)

In this passage, Jesus speaks to those that produce good moral works but at the same time, reject the kingdom of God. These people were good about cleaning up their lives on the outside for all to see (and expect the same "act" from others). In essence, Jesus was speaking to the "moralists" of that day. The moralists who rejected the only ONE who could truly change hearts, souls, and lives.

We as believers have done a good job of preaching morality without preaching Jesus. Our message should never be just about morality. Jesus' message was never about morality but about the kingdom of God.

An individual who simply "cleans up his act" opens the door for demons to come right in. What we need is true salvation that comes from Jesus Christ alone, not just mere morality. There are a lot of "good" and "moral" people that are still going to hell today because they can't get to Heaven without Jesus.

If we as believers are not careful, morality and religion can become a self-righteous seduction. This kind of seduction likes to deceive others into thinking that all is well with our relationship with God when it is not. As long as a person understands their sinful nature, they can be saved, daily. When a person is humble enough to understand their shortcomings, he is in a position to be delivered. It is when an individual becomes confident in their own righteousness that they believe they no longer are in need of a Savior, and that opens the door for all of hell to break loose.

My prayer for us today is that we can fully understand our need for Christ. He is the only one who can fill the empty voids in our life. We will either be the house that is occupied by demonic influence, or we will be the house that is fully occupied by Christ. A house that is fully occupied by Christ is not only a saved life, it is a changed one.

MAKING ASSUMPTIONS

"And the Lord said to Satan, From where do you come? And Satan (the adversary and the accuser) answered the Lord, From going to and fro on the earth and from walking up and down on it…So Satan went forth from the presence of the Lord and smote Job with loathsome *and* painful sores from the sole of his foot to the crown of his head.
And he took a piece of broken pottery with which to scrape himself, and he sat [down] among the ashes.
Then his wife said to him, Do you still hold fast your blameless uprightness? Renounce God and die!
But he said to her, You speak as one of the impious *and* foolish women would speak. What? Shall we accept [only] good at the hand of God and shall we not accept [also] misfortune *and* what is of a bad nature? In [spite of] all this, Job did not sin with his lips." (Job 2:2,7-10, AMP)

Often those who are closest to a person can be used by the Enemy to discourage and divert someone from the path of faith. Not only did Job's wife act foolishly during his time of distress but his three "friends" Eliphaz, Bildad, and Zophar (who initially were sent to comfort him), made it a point to attack and accuse Job of somehow sinning, thus assuming it *must* be the reason for his trepidation. However, their bitter advice and accusations were evidence of their lack of understanding and immature faith.

While the flame throwing of hardships revealed Job's true motives, it also exposed his companions' impure ones. Job's wife and friends failed him at a time when he needed them the most, making his suffering even greater as he faced it alone.

When companions are unable to comfort someone in need, it is most often due to their own feelings of insecurity and instability, often so consumed by their own fears that they are unable to find the strength and courage to be affirming and compassionate.

But scripture reveals to us that, "Job did not sin…" In fact, God was so pleased in how he handled the tragedies of his life, the assumptions of his accusers, and his unrelenting faithfulness to God that *"the Lord gave Job twice as much as he had before"* and *"the Lord blessed the latter days of Job more than his beginning…"*

So let every mature believer be careful in not jumping to assumptions even when things *clearly* appear to be a certain way. Job's friends applied a correct principle in the wrong manner by making the assumption that Job's suffering came as a result of his sin or disobedience to God. They erred as their assumptions were off based. May we as believers be comforters and have the wisdom and patience to resist making assumptions about others and situations we know little about.

Trust, Such a Complicated Ordeal

"Trust God from the bottom of your heart; don't
try to figure out everything on your own.
Listen for God's voice in everything you do, everywhere you go; he's
the one who will keep you on track. Don't assume that you know it
all. Run to God! Run from evil! Your body will glow with health,
your very bones will vibrate with life! Honor God with everything
you own; give him the first and the best. Your barns will burst,
your wine vats will brim over. But don't, dear friend, resent God's
discipline; don't sulk under his loving correction. It's the child he
loves that God corrects; a father's delight is behind all this."
(Proverbs 3:5-12, MSG)

The word "trust" seems to be such a simple word. It represents a "casting down" of the heavy weight on our shoulders and a "letting go" so to speak. However, human emotions makes the ability to trust such a complicated ordeal. Carrying life's exhaustive burdens at times seems much easier than trusting and letting go.

Even more difficult, is the ability to trust in a culture where we are taught to "take the bull by the horns", take control, and constantly strive to make things happen... it's counterintuitive. So we do everything possible to make sure the end result is what we desire, running over anyone who may stand in our way. It is a way of survival, especially for those who have felt the sting of disappointment, betrayal, or heartbreak. Friends, family members, co-workers, or even a spouse can leave one feeling vulnerable, despondent, and discouraged. However, it is at that very moment that we can choose to try to figure it all out, judge the perpetrator, become bitter, and distrustful of *everyone*. Or we can choose to trust God, waiting quietly, knowing His plans for us are of good and not of harm (Jeremiah 29:11).

When we genuinely trust The Lord, we can be at peace and rest in His promise.

During times when it is difficult to trust, we can take comfort in knowing Jesus is the ONE that can always be trusted. Be ever mindful of God and serve Him with a willing and obedient heart. When we trust Him out of a heart of obedience, He will remove the (stressful) obstacles of our life and make the crooked paths straight (Luke 3:5). He doesn't say when or how, He just promises that He will. As scripture points out, trusting God in His guidance brings physical well being, prosperity, and discipline. Although there are times of testing and hardship, rest assured that God still uses it for our good! (Romans 8:28).

There are many unknowns in life... employment, children's struggles, critical talk behind our backs, identity crisis, overwhelming debt, elderly parents to care for, and so much more. Let go *completely*. Take a chance and live life with an open heart. Being distrustful only leads to much lack and pain. Jesus promises He WILL work it all out. ALWAYS.

Arise and Shine

> "Arise [from the depression and prostration in which circumstances have kept you—rise to a new life]! Shine (be radiant with the glory of the Lord), for your light has come, and the glory of the Lord has risen upon you! For behold, darkness shall cover the earth, and dense darkness [all] peoples, but the Lord shall arise upon you [O Jerusalem], and His glory shall be seen on you. And nations shall come to your light, and kings to the brightness of your rising." (Isaiah 60:1-3, AMP)

Many believers often scoff or consider it "blasphemy" for one to even consider themselves to have any likeness to Christ. It is true that in and of ourselves, we are but mere flesh and have little "good" to offer. However, the good news is that if Christ resides in us today, then we too have access to everything He has access to. And yes, this includes His radiance! Had it not been so, than God would not command us to arise, shine, and be radiant with the glory of God!

All throughout scripture, the Lord's people are commanded to reflect HIS light. Believers are to be a witness to *all* the Nations. Does this seem too great of a task? Well beloved, you can begin being a light by reaching out to those around you at your local grocery store, the local park, or your local restaurant. I always say that you can impact the world by first impacting *your* world. Furthermore, scripture is clear that,

> "No one lights a lamp and hides it in a jar or puts it under a bed. Instead, he puts it on a stand, so that those who come in can see the light." (Luke 8:26, NIV)

It is to our detriment to try to hide our light or maintain it within our home or church environment. As God's Word depicts, we must GO and step out of our comfort zones. After all, the light of Christ within us is not for the Jew (believers) but for the Gentile (non-believers).

Before God's people go *anywhere*, we must first reflect the light of His glory. This is not something that is reflected merely by outward appearance but more importantly, reflected by the love and light of Jesus Christ we have in our hearts. True believers have both an inward and outward dimension of His radiance. As the world appears to gain greater in darkness, God's people should gain greater opportunity to shine ever so brightly.

The Lord resides in every believer and is the everlasting light for all His people so arise and shine, shine, shine.

TRUSTING GOD THROUGH BROKENHEARTEDNESS

> "I will bless the Lord at all times; His praise
> shall continually be in my mouth.
> My life makes its boast in the Lord; let the
> humble *and* afflicted hear and be glad.
> O magnify the Lord with me, and let us exalt His name together.
> I sought (inquired of) the Lord *and* required Him [of necessity
> and on the authority of His Word], and He heard me, and
> delivered me from all my fears. They looked to Him and were
> radiant; their faces shall never blush for shame *or* be confused."
> (Psalm 34:1-5, AMP)

This psalm was written during a time of David; when he pretended to be insane before Abimelech, who drove him out, and was forced to go away.

Biblical commentators suggest that Abimelech was fearful of David's authority, thus, causing him to drive David away. Though David knew his enemies wanted him dead and he experienced heartbreak, he trusted in God's divine protection and sovereignty over his life.

A "broken heart" is often experienced when there has been a "break" in a relationship or when one has suffered loss. Feelings of abandonment and betrayal can quickly begin to overwhelm the broken heart.

Scripture tells us that David "changed his behavior before them" (1 Samuel 21:13). Many people change or "alter" their behavior because of what has been done to them. Been hurt? Walls get built up. Been betrayed? Lack of trust begins to develop. Don't let people or unforeseen circumstances alter who you are. There is a joy that cannot be thieved when a believer chooses to trust in God.

Jesus said that it is *HIS* job to "heal the brokenhearted" (Is 61:1-3). One's heart can begin to beat again, live again, and love again when realized that healing comes from Christ alone.

David, even through times of loss and betrayal, continued to praise the Lord. The end result was a face that is radiant with victory rather than one that is shameful with defeat. Those rightly related to the Lord often suffer much affliction, however, those who seek the Lord will never lack the experience of God's goodness, even in difficult times.

Today I encourage you to choose to believe again. Choose to believe that God has a future purpose and plan for your life, regardless of circumstances or what has been done to you. Faith in the Lord does not mean that one is void of adversity. However, one can rest assured that ultimately, victory belongs to those who follow the Lord.

The Empty Tomb

"Early in the morning on the first day of the week, while it was still dark, Mary Magdalene came to the tomb and saw that the stone was moved away from the entrance. She ran at once to Simon Peter and the other disciple, the one Jesus loved, breathlessly panting, 'They took the Master from the tomb. We don't know where they've put him.' Peter and the other disciple left immediately for the tomb. They ran, neck and neck. The other disciple got to the tomb first, outrunning Peter. Stooping to look in, he saw the pieces of linen cloth lying there, but he didn't go in. Simon Peter arrived after him, entered the tomb, observed the linen cloths lying there, and the kerchief used to cover his head not lying with the linen cloths but separate, neatly folded by itself. Then the other disciple, the one who had gotten there first, went into the tomb, took one look at the evidence, and believed. No one yet knew from the Scripture that he had to rise from the dead. The disciples then went back home." (John 20:1-10, MSG)

Upon hearing Mary's story, Peter and John ran to the tomb. They expected to find the grave clothes gone, for they suspected a thief had stolen Jesus' body. To their astonishment, they found the shroud lying exactly where the body had been placed. The clothes still lay there, as if still around Jesus' body. Jesus was gone but the grave clothes…still there. The handkerchief used to cover Jesus' head was still in place where His head had laid. This puzzled Peter and John for they had not understood the power of the Resurrection that had taken place.

Notice, Mary went to the tomb EARLY, "while it was still dark". In doing so, she was the FIRST one to experience Jesus' working power. There is something that happens when we seek out Jesus early in the morning while it is still dark. Maybe it is the quietness of the morning or maybe a loving heart that seeks Him early in the morning compels Him to reveal Himself in such a powerful way.

Peter and John missed out. They too could have had a deeper understanding of the miraculous that was happening right before their very eyes but "they did not know the Scripture". But Mary knew... oh, she knew. So much so that at her discovery, she could not contain her excitement and RAN to share with the other disciples.

How many of us seek the Lord in the early morning hours, seeking Scripture, finding the miraculous in our lives? How many of us get so excited as God reveals Himself to us that we *run* to share with others? God's miraculous working power is happening everyday, in everything, all around us. We must seek and know the Scriptures to not only recognize it, but to understand it.

Today I encourage you to seek Jesus early in the morning. Let Him reveal himself to you through scripture and through others. He is dying to do it... yes, He wants to empower you and strengthen you throughout the day by constantly and consistently having communion with you.

"Perhaps we don't want to come face to face with the unsurrendered areas of our lives. We like our lives just as they are, even if it is less than God's best."

Does God Still Heal?

"As Jesus was walking along, he saw a man who had been born blind. His disciples asked him, 'Teacher, whose sin caused him to be born blind? Was it his own or his parents' sin?' Jesus answered, 'His blindness has nothing to do with his sins or his parents' sins. He is blind so that God's power might be seen at work in him. As long as it is day, we must do the work of him who sent me; night is coming when no one can work. While I am in the world, I am the light for the world.'"
(John 9:1-5, GNT)

Similarly to the testaments of old, much debate arises in Christian circles on whether or not God still heals and performs the miraculous today. Another posing question is, if so, then *who* does He choose to heal and *why*?

Blindness was common in Jesus' day. The Jews associated blindness (along with other infirmities) with sin. However, make no mistake, not every struggle or infirmity is due to sin.

If we observe the New Testament, we see that Jesus didn't heal everybody. He only healed those that God had sent Him to heal. "To heal", means to "restore to normal". Why did only certain ones get healed? So that the son of man would be glorified.

There have been several beautiful stories of many gaining eternal salvation through preachers' invitation of life through another's death at a funeral. Where does God get the greater glory? Healing one from a fatal disease or healing many through the death of one man? Was it not to God's greater glory to send *His* one and only son for the salvation of many?

God doesn't choose favorites. Our minds can't conceive God's greater plan. But realize this, whether someone's healing took place here on Earth or in

Heaven, both instances are for the glory of God. Even if someone passes from this life to the next, it is so that the son of God may be glorified.

At the end of the day, God's ways are greater than ours. We don't have to figure it all out. All we have to do is "be full of God and with that fullness, comes power"! Power to heal, power to save, and the power to gain greater understanding of His will and perspective.

A Heart of Courage

> "If you keep quiet at a time like this, help will come from heaven to the Jews, and they will be saved, but you will die and your father's family will come to an end. Yet who knows—maybe it was for a time like this that you were made queen!" (Esther 4:14, GNT)

Esther, who was an orphaned Jewess, often still saw herself as a lonely helpless child. Even after she became queen, she still battled feelings of fear, rejection, and insecurity. When faced with a trial during a time of desperation, Mordecai challenged her and compelled her with this question, "who knows if you have come to the kingdom for such a time as this?"

When God places us in a position of "privilege", there are a few things we should keep in mind:

- Although we may feel discouraged in our present circumstance. We know the ONE that gives us the courage to press on in obedience to the position He has set before us.
- A God given opportunity should not be taken lightly and should be viewed as an honor and privilege in humbleness and humility.
- No position of privilege overrides sound accountability and responsibility. In fact, there is great consequence to those who want to excuse disobedience or bad behavior because of their position.

Esther had done all the right things "physically" on the "outside" but now we would see if she was prepared "spiritually". We see this time and time again in our homes, in the workplace, and in our churches. Going through all the right steps, protocols, and looking good on the outside... but what is really going on in the inside? This is what matters most to God.

Esther's evidence of her strong faith and spiritual walk was revealed through her prayer, fasting, and devotion to God... even if that meant it would cost her life. She had the heart of a courageous lion and God used her fearless faith to accomplish His will. So how do you see yourself today? Do you see yourself as the rejected orphan? Or do you see yourself as the courageous lion, doing God's will no matter what the cost? Whatever God is calling you to do today, know that you were purposed for, "such a time as this".

Feminist?

> "Imitate me, then, just as I imitate Christ. I praise you because you always remember me and follow the teachings that I have handed on to you. But I want you to understand that Christ is supreme over every man, the husband is supreme over his wife, and God is supreme over Christ." (1 Corinthians 11:1-3, GNT)

Feminist movements for years have fought for equality in the workplace, in society, and in the home. Although it is clear that women are created in the image of God (Genesis 1:2), scripture is also clear about the specific roles men and women should have. The truth of the matter is, if we were really honest with ourselves, women CAN'T do all that a man can nor can a man do all that a woman can do. It simply goes against God's natural design.

Too often I have seen scripture and gender roles misused in order to control and manipulate. A godly woman shouldn't become defensive when people point out scripture about the appropriate role of a woman. However, at the same time, one shouldn't make the assumption that a woman doesn't know her appropriate role as a godly wife.

Certain groups of individuals quickly assume that today's Christian women do not maintain their appropriate role in the household. Why is this assumption made? It is simply because they believe a woman who knows her role should be (or at least appear to be) rendered powerless. This is the enemy's deception in many churches today. The truth is, God has given every believing woman His spirit so that she *can* walk in the fullness of His power!

Too often I see women in the church oppressed because they are not allowed to use the voice (or the gifts) that God has given them. Because of this, they soon become cold and embittered. Certainly not a joy to be around!

No doubt, women have been undervalued and underestimated, however, godly women should be concerned with where God says her proper role is, not what the feminist movement or well meaning (but misinformed) Christians say a woman's role is. Both can go to extremes (and frankly, quite often do). What does God say? Search the scriptures for yourselves.... it is filled with truth on this topic.

On the flip side, I have also seen many men who don't assume their appropriate role and positions because there was such an overpowering woman (typically a mom or wife) in their life that they weren't encouraged to be the man God called them to be. This is not only a detriment to the man but sadly enough, a detriment to the whole household.

In both cases, it is crippling and not as God intended it. God ordained proper gender roles in order to EMPOWER us, not to belittle us.

So, if you point out a "woman's" role, don't assume she doesn't like your pointing finger because she is a feminist. Maybe our quick pointing finger and judgmental assumptions could be a little "off-based".

The Bible does not support the degradation or abuse of women. At the same time, it does not support the right of women (or men) to put themselves above God's plan to do as they please and live a life against God's natural design.

FATHERLESS GENERATION

> "For as many as are led by the Spirit of God, these are sons of God. For you did not receive the spirit of bondage again to fear, but you received the Spirit of adoption by whom we cry out, "Abba, Father." The Spirit Himself bears witness with our spirit that we are children of God, and if children, then heirs—heirs of God and joint heirs with Christ, if indeed we suffer with *Him,* that we may also be glorified together."
> (Romans 8:14-17, NKJV)

It's a shame to see a fatherlessness generation growing rampant in America. Even individuals who have both parents living in the household often have "absentee" fathers. So many children either grow up without fathers or in dysfunctional families. They grow up insecure and unprotected, struggling to feel loved. The Bible says, "You don't have many fathers" (1 Corinthians 4:15). That person in our lives who helps us locate our identity and become who God intended us to be. Fathers serve their sons and daughters by helping them to discover who they are. In that, they gain security in their identity and and are not easily deterred when temptation comes their way. The growing epidemic of fatherless families has taken a grave toll on children, both young and old, in the form of emotional, social, spiritual, academic, physical, criminal, and suicidal issues later on in life. Fatherless children are twice as likely to drop out of school, experiment with drugs, and have increased odds for crime and incarceration.

The good news is... the Spirit of God enables every believer to call God "Abba, Father" or "Daddy" (v. 15). In fact, God revealed Himself throughout the Old Testament as "Father" (Jer 3:19). He *is* the perfect father who cares for each and every one of us. His love is greater than that of any earthly father. His love is perfect. Human fatherhood is imperfect however, God's love and plan for our lives never falls short.

Believers are God's children and we can be confident in knowing that we have been adopted into a *new* family. We no longer have to live a life of bondage but we can be secure in knowing that God has given us a Spirit of adoption. We are no longer orphans.

As adopted believers, we are new individuals beginning a new life. In the legal court system, the adopted individual gains all the rights as the one born into the family. They are legitimate heirs to the father's estate. In the same way, we all can enjoy what God has for us. He desires to share all good things with His children!

"Even if my father and mother abandon me, the LORD will hold me close."
(Psalm 27:10)

Leadership Roles and Responsibilities

"Now there was a man in Maon whose business was in Carmel, and the man was very rich. He had three thousand sheep and a thousand goats. And he was shearing his sheep in Carmel. The name of the man was Nabal, and the name of his wife Abigail. And she was a woman of good understanding and beautiful appearance; but the man was harsh and evil in his doings. He was of the house of Caleb."
(1 Samuel 25:2-3, NKJV)

Being in a position of leadership, albeit at home, church, or in the workplace is a great call and responsibility. Leadership, in any capacity requires personal growth and development, godly counsel and wisdom, and spiritual devotion. "Nabal", meaning "fool", was a man filled with pride known for being a tyrannical, oppressive leader.

A good leader must rid themselves of pride (which leads to destruction) and as Abigail, practice restraint and discretion while interacting with others and making decisions. Good, sound decisions are rarely made from "knee jerk" reactions or emotions. Abigail knew that she was a great woman of influence and her decisions would either lead to her husband's life or death (1 Samuel 25:23-35).

Essential ingredients for good leadership qualities include: mentorship, creativity, exhorting others, inspiring gifts and talents, expressing gratitude, and having a heart of humility and servant hood. A person in a leadership role must be adaptable to change and have a willingness to respect the thoughts and opinions of others.

While in a position of authority, it can be quite easy to focus on the task on hand and overlook the importance of *people*. People must be more important than roles, titles, or tasks. Self-sacrifice, gentleness, service without reward, patience, kindness, nurturing of relationships, mercy, grace--are all examples of qualifications that are necessary to be an effectual leader. Think that is too much to ask? It is indeed! Therefore, it is wise to take careful consideration prior to accepting a position of leadership. Most enjoy the recognition and glory but few are willing to work willingly and energetically for the sake of others, requesting nothing in return.

If you are someone who is in a leadership position today, consider this: Jesus was a leader who took on the role of a servant... expecting nothing yet giving us everything. This wasn't a sign of weakness but one of strength. Anyone can lead while expecting glitz and glory in return but it takes a great man of faith to serve out of a humble heart, expecting nothing. The Lord Himself exemplified these qualities, which is still necessary for all quality godly leaders today.

Hope Through Persecution

"But the high priest rose up and all who were his supporters, that is, the party of the Sadducees, and being filled with jealousy *and* indignation *and* rage, they seized and arrested the apostles (special messengers) and put them in the public jail. But during the night an angel of the Lord opened the prison doors and, leading them out, said, 'Go, take your stand in the temple courts and declare to the people the whole doctrine concerning this Life (the eternal life which Christ revealed).'"
(Acts 5:17-20, AMP)

The Bible reveals several accounts of persecution for the faith in both the Old and New Testaments. Persecutions against nations yes, however moreover, persecution towards individuals in particular. This regular occurrence of persecution came by way of not only the non-believers, but from the believing church.

The prophets were often persecuted because of their faith in God and their radical obedience to do His will. The twelve disciples were persecuted for taking a stand for the Lord (Matthew 5:11). Jesus himself suffered great persecution from the religious leaders of His day (John 5:16).

Persecution involves a type of harassment that is intended to inflict intense torment. Believers must be wise in discerning the true source of persecution and the motives that evoke it.

Peter's ministry attracted a lot of people. The Sadducees were controlled by jealousy that was fueled both by the apostles' popularity and by their own fears. Thus, they decided they must take action to stop the activity of Peter's ministry. The religious leaders tried to silence the apostles by arresting them and imprisoning them. However, not even the ironclad gates of the prison doors could keep the apostles down. The Lord opened the prison gates and commanded them to continue preaching the good news to all the people. How many of you know that when God is in the midst, no prison doors can keep you down. In Christ, not even death can keep you down!

This is the ultimate blessing that can be experienced in the midst of persecution, because God does not forsake the Christian facing persecution for the Kingdom's sake.

The Double-Minded Man

"If any of you is deficient in wisdom, let him ask of the giving God [Who gives] to everyone liberally *and* ungrudgingly, without reproaching *or* faultfinding, and it will be given him. Only it must be in faith that he asks with no wavering (no hesitating, no doubting). For the one who wavers (hesitates, doubts) is like the billowing surge out at sea that is blown hither *and* thither and tossed by the wind. For truly, let not such a person imagine that he will receive anything [he asks for] from the Lord, [For being as he is] a man of two minds (hesitating, dubious, irresolute), [he is] unstable *and* unreliable *and* uncertain about everything [he thinks, feels, decides]." (James 1:5-8, AMP)

A Christian who has not yet been made perfect in Christ constantly battles double-mindedness. He acts one way when he is with one group of people but acts another way when he is with another group of people. Or, he has a certain belief with one person but quickly changes his mind when he is in the presence of another person. This person, lacking in confidence, simply doesn't know who he is yet. He struggles with being insecure and spiritually immature.

James warns that the double-minded man will "not receive anything from the Lord". That's a strong statement! I don't know about you but I want to receive everything the Lord has in store for me.

To obtain the spiritual maturity necessary to avoid being a double-minded man, James urges believers to develop their faith by seeking wisdom from God. He reminds us that we have a choice: We could either give in to sin and suffer the consequences, or we can stand firm and experience the maturing of faith that comes by accepting the trials that will inevitably come. James maintained that the latter would produce patience and ultimately perfect and complete us in Christ (James 1:2-4).

The potential a Christian has for maturity relates to the realization of their God-given destiny, avoiding the striving that comes with reaching a goal that only God can enable us to achieve.

So today I urge you to be confident in the Lord and develop your faith by seeking wisdom from God, being stable in all your ways and avoiding the pitfall of being a double-minded believer.

Do Good to Please God

"Take care not to do your good deeds publicly *or* before men, in order to be seen by them; otherwise you will have no reward [reserved for and awaiting you] with *and* from your Father Who is in heaven. Thus, whenever you give to the poor, do not blow a trumpet before you, as the hypocrites in the synagogues and in the streets like to do, that they may be recognized *and* honored *and* praised by men. Truly I tell you, they have their reward in full already. But when you give to charity, do not let your left hand know what your right hand is doing, so that your deeds of charity may be in secret; and your Father Who sees in secret will reward you *openly*."
(Matthew 6:1-4, AMP)

The unchecked "do-gooder" and those operating with false motives is a detriment to the Holy Spirit. Those who do good things to be seen by men and want a "pat on the back" will receive no reward in Heaven. If we strive for anything, let us strive to do that which pleases God in accordance to our obedience to Him.

The "do-gooder" causes injury to both the leadership and the congregation. Leadership cannot wisely discern the heart and motives of the individual (nor do they want to) because the workhorse always says "yes" and the church needs people to step up into their *rightful* positions. However, what sometimes isn't recognized is that the do-gooder isn't interested in the well being of the leadership, nor are they interested in the well being of the congregation, they are not even interested in God's well-being and namesake. The "do-gooder" is interested in that one little sense of approval by man. That one little "pat on the back" in order to feel good about themselves, all the while missing what God truly has for them (even if seemingly it is something as simple as greeting a newcomer).

Now, with that being said, we as individuals in the congregation have a specific role we are to partake within the "family". We were never created to be benchwarmers on the pew. We were created to be an intrical moving part of the body. It is up to the individual to prayerfully consider what area they would serve in. It is pertinent that individuals get plugged into their passion otherwise, if out of alignment, the individual (along with the rest of the congregation) will be shaken and it will lead to disunity and discord. People must be plugged into their passion.

Often people are overwhelmed by too many things to do because there are so many telling them what they SHOULD do. One must determine how to appropriate their time according to how GOD says to appropriate time. Scripture gives us guidelines for God's proper order in prioritizing:

1) Your personal relationship with Jesus Christ
2) Your commitment to home and family
3) Your service to God through ministry and church involvement

Many get this confused. Quite often, that is when we hear the shocking news of the elder robbing the tithe, the pastor leaving his wife, or the Sunday school teacher who doesn't want anything to do with the church anymore.

People's motives and priorities are out of balance. In order for the church body to run as a well-oiled machine, church members must be aligned in their *proper* position. More importantly, this will allow for God to get the glory He deserves, not the "pat on the back" the do-gooder thinks they deserve.

DRUNKENNESS AND GLUTTONY LEADS TO POVERTY

> "Don't associate with people who drink too much wine or stuff themselves with food. Drunkards and gluttons will be reduced to poverty. If all you do is eat and sleep, you will soon be wearing rags." (Proverbs 23:20-21, GNT)

Often drunkenness is visualized as laughter, partying, and having fun. However, the reality is that drunkenness leads to strife, quarrels, anxiety, and poor health. Think about how many marriages, homes, jobs, and businesses have been destroyed due to an enslavement of drugs and alcohol.

Although gluttony is also a type of enslavement, it is perhaps, more acceptable in our society. Similarly to drugs and alcohol, it is a craving that cannot be satisfied. It too can have devastating effects on a person's health. Proverbs 23:2 says, "…put a knife to your throat if you are a man given to appetite".

Although it may seem harsh, Solomon, in essence was trying to make a point by saying if we don't have control in this area of our lives, chances are we won't have control when it comes to the more severe circumstances of our lives.

So what is *gluttony*? Living in a country where food is rich and plentiful, this may be a little more difficult to recognize. Dictionary.com describes gluttony as *"a person who eats or drinks excessively"* or *"a person with a remarkably great desire for something"*. However, gluttony is not limited to food only. For example, some people may continually make self-destructing choices because they are *"a glutton for punishment"*.

Substance abuse and yes, even food is used by many as a way to escape from reality and omit dealing with the emotional pain caused by either themselves or by others.

The same sins of Sodom and Gomorrah are prevalent in our society today. We have lost our way in reveling with everything in excess.

Whether it's a struggle with gluttony, alcohol or substance abuse, the root of the cause is all the same…an overwhelming desire to attempt in satisfying the flesh.

The good news is that God is in the business of bringing forgiveness, wholeness, and healing to each person's life. Recognizing His sovereignty brings a person out of bondage and quite frankly, is the only way to begin a road of recovery and victory.

OBEDIENCE REWARDED

> "Behold, I set before you this day a blessing and a curse—
> The blessing if you obey the commandments of the
> Lord your God which I command you this day;
> And the curse if you will not obey the commandments of the Lord
> your God, but turn aside from the way which I command you
> this day to go after other gods, which you have not known.
> (Deuteronomy 11:26-28, AMP)

Obedience to God is the key to His continued blessings (Deuteronomy 6:6-9). Even if at times it means yielding our own goals and expectations. There is no use in running to someone else for advice who has no idea what you are going through or what your future holds. God alone sees the greater picture. We must be obedient to Him, even when it goes against what we personally desire to do.

The chastening of the Lord is for the purpose of instructing His people for their betterment. It is through His chastening that we learn discipline that reaps noble and upright character. God's dealings with us are always designed to teach us about His holiness and prepare us for our destiny.

To disobey God is to have a "hard heart" or a "stiff neck". This includes resisting the Holy Spirit and being rebellious against the Lord. Rebellion leads to calamity. A hardened heart is one that has become unfeeling, unsympathetic, stubborn and calloused. The Vine's Concise dictionary describes "hard" as being dry and difficult. Ever known anyone like that? Difficult, hardened people are not pleasant to be around. They hardened their hearts as a defense mechanism, however, this only leads to further anger, bitterness, and resentment. Soon thereafter, they isolate themselves and become consumed with overwhelming feelings of distrust and begin to believe the lie that everyone is out to get them. The truth of God's word can no longer penetrate into their spirit. However, God intended for us to bless and be blessed by Him and by other people. The hardened heart only further injures themselves. Hardened people no longer have faith in God or in others. However, faith or trust in God is essential to receiving all God has for their life.

If we earnestly obey the Lord, He promises to give us an abundance of blessings, which includes rain for our land that we may gather a harvest and have enough grass in our fields for our livestock, that we may eat and be satisfied. (Deuteronomy 11:13-15).

Undeserved Mercy and Grace

"Among these we as well as you once lived *and* conducted ourselves in the passions of our flesh [our behavior governed by our corrupt and sensual nature], obeying the impulses of the flesh and the thoughts of the mind [our cravings dictated by our senses and our dark imaginings]. We were then by nature children of [God's] wrath *and* heirs of [His] indignation, like the rest of mankind. But God—so rich is He in His mercy! Because of *and* in order to satisfy the great *and* wonderful *and* intense love with which He loved us, Even when we were dead (slain) by [our own] shortcomings *and* trespasses, He made us alive together in fellowship *and* in union with Christ; [He gave us the very life of Christ Himself, the same new life with which He quickened Him, for] it is by grace (His favor and mercy which you did not deserve) that you are saved (delivered from judgment and made partakers of Christ's salvation). And He raised us up together with Him and made us sit down together [giving us joint seating with Him] in the heavenly sphere [by virtue of our being] in Christ Jesus (the Messiah, the Anointed One)." (Ephesians 2:3-6, AMP)

"Mercy" is not giving a person what they deserve (in this case, judgment). It's like a judge finding you guilty, but then withholding any punishment. We cannot earn nor are we worthy of God's underserved mercy but He extends it to us because of His great love for us.

To fully understand God's mercy, one must understand God's grace. Grace is getting *more* than one deserves. It's like that same judge awarding you with a large lump sum of money *after* you were found guilty!

Now, is God's grace a free ticket for us to sin? Absolutely not. In fact, the inverse is recognizing our need for God's grace. He delights in bestowing divine favor upon us. This should want to keep us from sin all the more. It's God's kindness that leads us to repentance! (Romans 2:4).

In order to exude mercy and grace, believers should exhibit compassion and empathy towards one another. We should identify ourselves with the suffering of another brother or sister.

God's mercy and grace is greater than sin. His mercy and grace are enormous, boundless, and is available to everybody and anybody. Believers have been forgiven, sins have been forgotten, and we get the privilege of experiencing God's mercy and grace not only in Heaven, but *right now* as we live here on Earth.

A Submitted Heart

"Obey your spiritual leaders and submit to them [continually recognizing their authority over you], for they are constantly keeping watch over your souls *and* guarding your spiritual welfare, as men who will have to render an account [of their trust]. [Do your part to] let them do this with gladness and not with sighing *and* groaning, for that would not be profitable to you [either]." (Hebrews 13:17, AMP)

Many Christians today "cringe" at the sound of the word "submit", especially women. Unfortunately, the word has gained a bad rep as many people in authority have misused and abused scripture in order to gain power and manipulate and control their subordinates.

To "submit" doesn't mean you must be subservient to a spirit of tyranny (which is what the abuser becomes). Tyranny gains power through constant disapproval and abuse of its subjects. Those under its power labor tirelessly under the false hope that one day they will please their master and be rewarded. Hoping that FINALLY they can feel whole, happy, free, and loved. But the taskmaster is never pleased; he refuses to be because in doing so, he must give up power. Therefore, those in submission under it, will continue to strive for an acceptance they will never receive. Does that sound like the kind of submission the Lord intended? I think not. In fact, in regards to a marriage, Ephesians 5:25-28 commands that husbands love their wives like Christ loved the church. Did Christ love the church with manipulation and control? Absolutely not. Scripture gives us specific instructions on how we must act during our prospective roles in order that there may be a supreme cohesiveness…powerful! It is difficult for this to work well when one refuses to lead as God intended or when one refuses to submit as God instructed.

To submit doesn't mean you can't have an opinion or a brain. It doesn't mean that you are a doormat. It simply means that you withdraw, avoiding a "fight", trusting in God, and giving those in authority permission to lead. Stepping aside, submitting our flesh, and letting others lead is such a powerful gesture. God can do the miraculous through a submitted heart. Therein which, His power and glory may be revealed through you.

Proper roles of authority and submission isn't merely limited to roles between a husband and wife, it also pertains to our proper roles in the church, in the workplace, and within the community. Together we are all on a mission (ie subMISSION).

Spiritual Parenting

"To Timothy, a true son in the faith: Grace, mercy, *and* peace from God our Father and Jesus Christ our Lord." (1 Timothy 1:2)

In Paul's letters to Timothy and Titus, we often see that he refers to them as "a true son" or "beloved son". This may appear strange as Paul never married and had no children. However, Paul spent a significant amount of time admonishing and teaching the younger men in his life the ways of Christ.

Spiritual parenting is vital in the Christian church today. Spiritually mature men and women have a responsibility to mentor those that are less mature in the faith. The mature men in the Christian church should encourage the younger men and likewise, the more mature women should encourage the younger women. The aged Christian should lead by example and teach the younger generation the word of God. The spiritual parent must not only be mature in years but most importantly, mature in their walk with Christ. To be *mature* means to be "fully grown" or "fully developed". A spiritual parent or mentor should be fully grown *spiritually*.

Spiritual parents should train the "spiritual child" by using the same grace God uses in bringing salvation to all men and women. Ephesians 6:4 states, *"Fathers, do not exasperate your children; instead, bring them up in the training and instruction of the Lord."* Mentors should be careful not to irritate or worsen the pain that a younger Christian may be experiencing. The aged Christian should exercise their authority by extending grace when the spiritual child errs. The less mature Christian has not yet been freed from doing what the flesh pleases.

Many children mimic the same behavioral patterns they see their parents representing within the home. Similarly, a spiritual child will model exactly what they see the spiritual parent doing within the church. Therefore, a spiritual parent must be one that models godly mannerisms, characteristics, and conduct. They should have reverent behavior and godly conversation. In this present age, it is crucial that the more mature Christian teaches the younger Christians to live soberly and righteously.

Having spiritual parents in the church will also give the younger generation an opportunity to find God's purpose and calling on their life, including their call in the ministry. Who knows, the spiritual parent may even receive a sweet surprise when they gain knowledge of a new skill set taught from the younger generation of the spiritual child.

Man's Discipline vs God's Discipline

"Our fathers disciplined us for a little while as they thought best; but God disciplines us for our good, that we may share in his holiness. No discipline seems pleasant at the time, but painful. Later on, however, it produces a harvest of righteousness and peace for those who have been trained by it" (Hebrews 12:10, 11 NIV).

Notice the above scripture points out that God disciplines us for our good. I know... the thought of the word "discipline" makes many of us cringe. Partly, because it has been so abused and misused in Christian circles (even well-meaning individuals simply lack the spiritual maturity to know how to use it appropriately). Many have used the above scripture as a license to judge, criticize, point fingers, and speak harshly about and to one another. I like what I heard one pastor say, "When you point one finger, notice that you have three pointing right back at you."

The scripture says GOD disciplines. Why then are we so overly consumed with chastising one another? Although it is wise to receive good counsel (Proverbs 15:22, Proverbs 1:5, Proverbs 12:15), one must discern and consider the source. Discipline from man must come from a genuine place of love (not from a place of offense, insecurity, the need to control, jealousy, self-righteousness, a critical spirit, etc). None of the aforementioned characteristics are from God. It is crucial that we discern between human fragility in their mistakes to discipline and the perfect knowledge of our heavenly Father, who seeks our profit, and cannot err in how He disciplines. Use discretion when seeking wise counsel.

As painful as it may be at times, God's discipline always results in a better you. It is the pinnacle of why He desires to discipline us. It is also important to recognize that God's correction is not condemnation; it is to promote holiness.

Although we see many instances in the bible where God used what we would consider "harsh measures" to discipline His people, it was done so due to sin and rebellion (not due to lack of perfectionism). Nonetheless, God is our Creator and He is Sovereign over all. How and when God chooses to discipline His people is God's business and we should never try to take God's place by making it ours.

For those who have felt the sting of being "disciplined" in a godless manner, know that that too can be used for your good. Maybe the experience will grow your heart into a heart of compassion for those who genuinely need it. Maybe it is simply a lesson on how not to treat others.

Man may sometimes chasten us, to gratify their fleshly passions. But God, the Creator of our souls never willingly grieves nor afflicts his children. It is always for our profit. Let us then use discernment when it comes to the afflictions brought on us by the malice of men, and that brought to us by our wise and gracious Father who does so out of love and for our eternal good.

STEADY MY HEART

"For the righteous will never be moved;
he will be remembered forever. He is not afraid of bad news;
his heart is firm, trusting in the Lord. His
heart is steady; he will not be afraid,
until he looks in triumph on his adversaries. He has distributed
freely; he has given to the poor; his righteousness endures forever;
his horn is exalted in Honor. The wicked man sees it and is angry;
he gnashes his teeth and melts away;
the desire of the wicked will perish!" (Psalm 112:6-10, ESV)

The wicked often seek to fulfill their appetites with accusations, intimidation, bullying, betrayal, and victimizing others. Their actions defy the living God and they take no account of Him or His Word.

Envy, slander, gossip, and all manner of evil can be overwhelming to God's people. However, Believers whose hearts are steadfast in The Lord can not be easily shaken. We know we can trust and rely on The Lord. A man in right standing with The Lord can have a settled spirit. We need not to fear or be intimidated when evil appears to have its way and prosper. It takes great effort to keep our minds upon The Lord when our world seems to be collapsing. However, when we keep our eyes on Jesus, we will remain calm and undisturbed. Furthermore, we can take confidence in knowing that Godliness will lead to a life of blessedness whereas wickedness will lead to a life of destruction.

So what is this blessed life? It is a life where in the darkest hours of affliction and trial, the light of hope and peace springs up within us. It is a life where seasonable mourning turns into eternal joy and dancing. It is a life where we have the privilege of learning from Christ's example. It is a life where it is effortless to do good. It is a life where He turns a once stoney heart into a heart of compassion that uses discretion while dealing with others.

Trusting in the Lord is the best and surest way of establishing our heart. It is this type of joy and confidence that is the envy of the wicked. But rest assured that the desire of the wicked and their seemingly ways of prospering will perish.

God did not intend for us to have a frantic, stressed out life. He wants us to make the most of our time while here on earth but He wants us to be overcomers, not overwhelmers. Even those whom we think are never shaken question why certain things happen in their life. To be steady or steadfast means to be firm and secure, knowing that as Believers, we are firmly seated in Heavenly places and have a strong support, a firm foundation, and strength that comes from Christ alone.

So today I encourage you to not be shaken. Do not fret. Keep your heart firm and steady knowing that you can trust in The Lord. Be confident and rejoice in knowing that God promises in due time, the righteous will obtain more honor than the wicked.

FLESH VS SPIRIT

"For those who are according to the flesh and are controlled by its unholy desires set their minds on and pursue those things which gratify the flesh, but those who are according to the Spirit and are controlled by the desires of the Spirit set their minds on and seek those things which gratify the [Holy] Spirit. Now the mind of the flesh [which is sense and reason without the Holy Spirit] is death [death that comprises all the miseries arising from sin, both here and hereafter]. But the mind of the [Holy] Spirit is life and [soul] peace [both now and forever]. [That is] because the mind of the flesh [with its carnal thoughts and purposes] is hostile to God, for it does not submit itself to God's Law; indeed it cannot. So then those who are living the life of the flesh [catering to the appetites and impulses of their carnal nature] cannot please or satisfy God, or be acceptable to Him."
(Romans 8:5-8, AMP)

Quite often the people that tempt our flesh the most is the person we see in the mirror everyday. As Christians, we should have an honest evaluation of ourselves daily. We should grieve over our own spiritual shortcomings. Not as a way to walk in condemnation but as a way to carry ourselves as imitators of Christ. True character is often revealed when life's circumstances do not go our way. How do we respond during these troubling times? Are we reactive in our flesh? Always acting on impulse? Or are we proactive in tackling obstacles in a Christ-like manner?

Daily we battle with two mindsets... that of the flesh and that of the Spirit. The mindset of the flesh leads to death whereas the mindset of the Spirit leads to life and peace.

We can do a self evaluation of our daily walks with Christ by assessing these characteristics and see where we fall on the richter scale, so to speak.

The sinful nature focuses on pleasing the flesh, is hostile towards God, does not follow the leading of the Holy Spirit, is in rebellion against God, does not abide by the law of God, and cannot please God.

The spiritual nature focuses on the leading of the Holy Spirit, pursues peace, abides by God's law, is one with Christ, and gives everlasting life.

Although abiding by the Law cannot save us from sin, Christians can live a victorious life where we achieve victory over our carnal nature. The struggle against our flesh will continue throughout our life here on Earth. The question is, are we being led by our flesh or by God's Spirit? Catering to the flesh is unacceptable to God... that's a strong statement!

So let's take some time today and look in the mirror and have an honest evaluation of ourselves. There is no condemnation for those that are in Christ Jesus (Romans 8:1)... but oh what joy, peace, and life awaits those that desire to be led by God's Spirit!

WORSHIP THE CREATOR, NOT HIS CREATION

"How can we describe God? With what can we compare him? With an idol? An idol made from a mold, overlaid with gold, and with silver chains around its neck? The man too poor to buy expensive gods like that will find a tree free from rot and hire a man to carve a face on it, and that's his god—a god that cannot even move!
Are you so ignorant? Are you so deaf to the words of God—the words he gave before the world began? Have you never heard nor understood? It is God who sits above the circle of the earth. (The people below must seem to him like grasshoppers!) He is the one who stretches out the heavens like a curtain and makes his tent from them. He dooms the great men of the world and brings them all to naught. They hardly get started, barely take root, when he blows on them and their work withers, and the wind carries them off like straw.
'With whom will you compare me? Who is
my equal?' asks the Holy One."
(Isaiah 40:18-25, TLB)

Most people who have any concept of idolatry probably think of pagans bowing down and worshipping a strange-looking idol—a carved image or statue. That's part of what idolatry means, but since that is not part of our everyday culture, how do God's commands against idolatry apply to Believers today?

Idolatry is not just venerating a statue, carving or painting. Idolatry occurs when we begin to value anything more than we value God. Whatever is greatly admired, loved, or revered... heroes, heroines, star, superstars, icons, celebrities, beloved pets, family members, careers, position, ministries, titles, drugs, alcohol, food, vanity, money, heartthrobs, houses, cars... anything that is more thought of or more revered than God is an idol.

If we spend more time thinking about our hero than God, that's idolatry. If our every thought is about the latest gadget or our personal appearance, that's idolatry. If the first priority in our lives is our family, even that's idolatry.

Make no mistake, none of the people, things or false gods can save us. They cannot satisfy or sustain us. They cannot compare to our Maker and our Creator who knows our ins and outs… who knows every hair on our head (Luke 12:7).

Isaiah expresses strong antagonism against these false gods through his sarcasm, satire, and denunciation of them. He further denotes the folly that will come to anyone who worships false idols.

How about you today? Is there anything in your life that causes you to think more upon that thing than God? It really doesn't matter how big or small the "thing" is. Regardless, it can hinder our ability to have an intimate relationship with God. Pull out the pen and pad. Make a list of what those things may be. Allow God to show you and ask HIM to be the one to fill the voided places in your life.

God Loves Those that Struggle with Their Sexuality Too

> "Now therefore, it is already an utter failure for you that you go to law against one another. Why do you not rather accept wrong? Why do you not rather let yourselves be cheated? No, you yourselves do wrong and cheat, and you do these things to your brethren! Do you not know that the unrighteous will not inherit the kingdom of God? Do not be deceived. Neither fornicators, nor idolaters, nor adulterers, nor homosexuals, nor sodomites, nor thieves, nor covetous, nor drunkards, nor revilers, nor extortioners will inherit the kingdom of God. And such were some of you. But you were washed, but you were sanctified, but you were justified in the name of the Lord Jesus and by the Spirit of our God."
> (1 Corinthians 6:7-11 New King James Version, NKJV)

Paul identifies two kinds of sexual immoral persons here: "adulterers" and "men who have sex with men" (in Romans 1:26 he adds the category of women who practice homosexuality). God, however, does save and sanctify people like those described in the above scripture. Why is it then that it is so easy to "overlook" some sin and concentrate on the sins of a certain group of people, like homosexuals for example. Let's face it, most of us have struggled with one or more of the above mentioned sins (maybe still do). Why is it easier to receive the thief, the gossip, and the drunkard but not the adulterer or homosexual? Do you know Jesus died for him too? Do you know that God loves them too? If "while we were yet still sinners Christ died for us" (Romans 5:8) how much more should the body of Christ love and forgive homosexuals and adulterers and point them to Christ?

Christians have done a very good job of hating certain kinds of groups and have made it very clear that they would not be welcomed in our homes, workplace, community, and our church. That is *not* the heart of Jesus. Isn't that what the church is for? Has the Christian community become so arrogant in our "good works" that we have lost sight of this? Jesus said, "I did not come for the well, but for the sick". Yet Christians who are supposed to be "Christ-like" say, "I do not come for the sick, but for the well." We have failed.... failed miserably. We have hidden from the very world God has called us to be a light to and we have shunned the very people that God wants us to love... the "sick".

The love walk of a Christian has become a crucial battleground. We have confused becoming "haters" of sin with becoming "haters" of people. We will one day have to hold an account to God for turning people away from the church, away from Him instead of pointing people to the church, and to Christ.

There is an ALL OUT WAR for the lives of worldly people, yes - even homosexuals. Will you help push them to hell or will you point them to heaven? If the church is going to be "homophobic", then we must not be hypocritical and we must become "fat-phobic", "lust-phobic", "gossiper-phobic", "pride-phobic", "arrogant-phobic", "smoker-phobic", and "whatever else-phobic". The result? An empty church. What is it that you struggle with today?

Overall, scripture advocates that human beings are more then just sexual or physical beings. It's about winning souls. God is interested in the wholeness of broken people as well as in every Christians' wholeness (which encompasses every area of our life). So next time you encounter someone who struggles with something like homosexuality, just remember, God loves them too.

He Will Turn it All Around

"I called out to you, God; I laid my case before you:
'Can you sell me for a profit when I'm dead?
auction me off at a cemetery yard sale? When I'm 'dust to dust' my songs
and stories of you won't sell. So listen! and be kind! Help me out of this!'
You did it: you changed wild lament into whirling dance;
You ripped off my black mourning band and decked me with
wildflowers. I'm about to burst with song; I can't keep quiet
about you. God, my God, I can't thank you enough."
(Psalm 30:8-12, MSG)

In a world where we have access to many "drive-thru" luxuries and everything seems to be going well, it can become easy to forget God our Creator. We begin to fail in our dependance on God.

Often as Christians, we can grow secure in our arrogance, forget our God, and begin to rely more on worldly methods in lieu of God's methods. Shattered strength and self-reliance that has been swept away calls us to cry out for God's mercy. God is not the author of our turmoil but sometimes He allows it so we may become reliant on Him and see His gracious deliverance.

God does not delay in answering us... but He does so in His perfect timing. The Psalmist David was so grateful to God for turning things around in his life, that he couldn't help giving God the praise He long deserved. He replaced his wailing and sackcloth for dancing and joy.

It is during our most difficult circumstances that we beckon to God relentlessly and cling on to the only One that can gives us hope, and turn things around in the midst of stormy situations. It is during calamity that we turn to God for help, and God is faithful to hear our prayers.

I don't know what you are going through today and cannot begin to describe the great varieties of pain you may be experiencing. Maybe it's the stomach-turning kind, the urge to bolt kind, the need to hide kind, or maybe the need to medicate kind. No matter how agonizing (and to our dismay and disappointment), self-reliant methods doesn't make it all go away. After trying to handle it on our own, we become devastated over the realization that all of our attempts have been futile and the pain is very much still alive in our lives. The good news is that your pain is not a life sentence. God will turn it all around. Difficult experiences do come to an end and a joyful morning follows a period of sorrow.

INCASED BY GRACE

"For no one is put right in God's sight by doing what the Law requires; what the Law does is to make us know that we have sinned. But now God's way of putting people right with himself has been revealed. It has nothing to do with law, even though the Law of Moses and the prophets gave their witness to it. God puts people right through their faith in Jesus Christ. God does this to all who believe in Christ, because there is no difference at all: everyone has sinned and is far away from God's saving presence. But by the free gift of God's grace all are put right with him through Christ Jesus, who sets them free."
(Romans 3:20-24, GNT)

Did you catch that? "Everyone has sinned..." Yes, everyone. Your pastor, your preacher, your priest, the sweet little old lady behind the piano, your momma, your papa, your mentor, your teacher, your idol, your child... everyone.

Having shown that all (Jew and Gentile) are unrighteous, Paul explains that we are saved by the saving grace of Jesus Christ alone. Trying to obtain righteousness by simply observing the law is impossible. God says if we even think of someone wrongfully, then we are already guilty of sin (Matthew 5:28). Furthermore, if we claim to be without sin, then we deceive ourselves (1 John 1:8).

Sin is often easily identified by deeds such as murder, lying, stealing, cheating, etc. However, deep within the human heart underlies all sin, especially the attitude of, "I know better than God in this matter".

A lot of us don't understand how truly loved by God we are. Thus, we try to earn His "good graces" and "favor" through exhaustive works. Many Christians would proudly put the title, "Biblical Scholar" onto their resume. However, the truth is extensive biblical knowledge can easily be overshadowed by how someone lives out their lives, revealing what they truly believe about themselves and God.

Most often than not, Believers sit themselves on the "victim's seat" (taking on a vow of poverty, punishment, exhaustive works, etc). Well meaning Christians do this "all in the name of Christ" and all the while Christ is beckoning us to sit with Him on the "mercy seat" (experiencing compassion, forgiveness, freedom from punishment or harm). We need to see ourselves free in Christ and say to the things (or people) that would try to keep us in bondage, "No longer!" It's okay to say, "yes" to the good things of God (really, it is) and to be confident people of God.

Most people in ministry fear touching the topic of "grace" because they think it will give God's people a license to sin. Grace is power *from* sin, not permission *to* sin. In other words, grace gives us the power to not *want* to sin. After all, have you heard? It's His loving kindness that brings us to repentance (Romans 2:4).

The Ultimate Love Story

> "For God so loved the world, that He gave His only begotten Son, that whoever believes in Him shall not perish, but have eternal life."
> (John 3:16, NIV)

There's a new buzz in town. Have you heard about it? He is the man every woman has been dying to see. He is every woman's love interest. Women everywhere are enticed by this handsome, successful, and charming man. The man every woman has been waiting for is portrayed in every romance novel, love film, and Disney movie. However, these popular fictional characters are not what God intends for us and are often far from being godly.

Every woman dreams of having the type of romance where a man will pursue her and take her to a place where she has never been. But the truth is, this fantasy is just a counterfeit of the real deal... it's just... well... a fantasy.

We live in a world that is awestricken with love stories. But they are not love stories at all - they are just lust stories, sex-fantasy stories, and violent domination stories. Even as young men and women, before we began to have any knowledge about our bodies, we were fed lies about what true love is. Experiencing the perverse version of love is hard enough, but even more dangerous, it ultimately hinders our love and intimacy with God.

The *truth* is that God *is* love. The man every woman has *really* been dying to see has already died for you and me on the cross 2000 years ago. That man's name is Jesus! With outstretched arms on the cross, HE made the ultimate sacrifice. HE gave the most selfless act of love. HE is the one that took the most violent of beatings so that he may live with you for eternity. When God said "I will love you forever", HE meant it! YOU are HIS love interest. There is no "forever" that is greater than eternity.

Everyday, worldly men (and women) make promises they don't intend to keep just so they can get what they want (if you know what I mean). And the fictional characters we are inundated with on a daily basis are *no different*.

I encourage you today to read a real love story. It is the story of God's love for you and for me. If you have never read the Bible, start in the book of Hosea. It will "wow" you!

Hosea is a prophet of love, but not the kind of perverse love the world feeds us. It is an astonishing romantic love story that parallels God's love for His people. Hosea is commanded to marry a common prostitute and have children with her... well, I don't want to give away the story so you will just have to read it for yourself.

God loves us, chases us, and pursues us at our worst. He keeps us after He gets us and shows us what real love is all about. Knowing this type of love will cure any desires for distortions of love that keeps us from loving the God who first loved us.

The Problem with the Message of Prosperity

"I'm glad in God, far happier than you would ever guess—happy that you're again showing such strong concern for me. Not that you ever quit praying and thinking about me. You just had no chance to show it. Actually, I don't have a sense of needing anything personally. I've learned by now to be quite content whatever my circumstances. I'm just as happy with little as with much, with much as with little. I've found the recipe for being happy whether full or hungry, hands full or hands empty. Whatever I have, wherever I am, I can make it through anything in the One who makes me who I am. I don't mean that your help didn't mean a lot to me—it did. It was a beautiful thing that you came alongside me in my troubles." (Philippians 4:10-14, MSG)

Many well-meaning Christians try to lure people into receiving Christ by promising a prosperous life. Although the Gospel *does* promise us the good news of salvation from eternal damnation (and there is no better news than that!), the falsehood that everything in life will be prosperous is contrary to God's word. In fact, Christ promises, *"Here on earth you will have many trials and sorrows; but cheer up, for I have overcome the world."* (John 16:33, TLB).

The problem with the message of prosperity is that many Christian circles use it as a means to compare lives and say, *"If you are in lack, then you MUST be doing something wrong!"* To bring such accusations is nonsensical. This type of mindset really comes from a pompous attitude. To think someone is righteous in their own strength is arrogance. If someone seemingly has a "perfect life", then it is by God's grace *alone*.

God weeps and hurts with us when we go through struggles and trials of every kind. This is the product of living in a fallen and sinful world.

However, *it is up to God* and His business *alone* in what areas we will (or will *not*) "prosper" in.

Paul had it right. Whether he had much or had little, it did not define who he was; nor did it deter him from keeping the faith. Some believers shame the rich, some shame the poor. Some believers accuse the "little" faith of the sick, some accuse the faith to get well. Whether rich or poor, healthy or sick, it should not bring shame or arrogance. We as Christians must be stripped of self-entitlements and learn how to be confident and content in *all* circumstances.

To be *content*, simply means to be satisfied in wherever you are in your life today. Even our trials can be turned for God's glory (and that's certainly something to celebrate)! How about you? Where are you in your life today? My hope is that you can be as content and confident as Paul and say, "I'm just as happy with little as with much, with much as with little."

Don't Take the Master's Body to a Brothel

"There's more to sex than mere skin on skin. Sex is as much spiritual mystery as physical fact. As written in Scripture, 'The two become one.' Since we want to become spiritually one with the Master, we must not pursue the kind of sex that avoids commitment and intimacy, leaving us more lonely than ever—the kind of sex that can never "become one." There is a sense in which sexual sins are different from all others. In sexual sin we violate the sacredness of our own bodies, these bodies that were made for God-given and God-modeled love, for "becoming one" with another. Or didn't you realize that your body is a sacred place, the place of the Holy Spirit? Don't you see that you can't live however you please, squandering what God paid such a high price for? The physical part of you is not some piece of property belonging to the spiritual part of you. God owns the whole works. So let people see God in and through your body."
(1 Corinthians 6:16-20, MSG)

As part of the human race, we are created to love and *be* loved. It is a natural desire to want to feel accepted, wanted, and needed. However, when those desires become stronger than our desire to pursue God, we become void of His purity. The consequence is a path that leads to spiritual death. To be spiritually dead is to be separated from God. Do not be deceived into thinking that the fight against sexual impurity is simply confined to the world or to the non-believer. Indeed it is not. Shockingly, it is all too prevalent within the house of God. Believers often abandon all Biblical knowledge and God's ways when life becomes too much to bear. Many get tired of waiting on God and decide to do things *their* way. The result? A broken spirit and a lonely body. Dawn breaks and the sobering realization that you are no longer needed for your sexual advancements closes in on your already vulnerable and insecure being. Simply put, you've been tossed out with today's trash.

We live in a broken sinful world that is cruel and unpredictable. There are many outside factors that make life very difficult. The temptation for a "quick fix" or a chance encounter for a little satisfaction makes it all the more enticing. However, this kind of fleeting "love" can never fully gratify. We are created to pursue a love that only God can fulfill. Yes, even within the confines of marriage, there is a kind of love that God alone can satisfy.

Sex outside of marriage may feel good for a moment, but the repercussion of allowing our bodies to be sexually used and abused has long-lasting effects. It can take a lifetime for the scars of the emotional, physical, spiritual, and mental wounds to heal (if they heal at all).

While feeling the weight of the world on our shoulders, remaining sexually pure *is* a constant battle. We are at war against the fiery darts of a sexual society enticed by lewd music, explicit films, provocative advertisements, and the "Kimye's" of our culture.

We are created in and are a part of the image of God. Should we then allow our bodies to mimic that of a prostitute or brothel? I think not. The only way to escape the sin of sexual immorality is to come to Jesus through faith, drawn by the Holy Spirit. Faith in Christ leads to spiritual life, and ultimately to *eternal* life. Let God be the one to fulfill your desires to *be* and *feel* loved. I promise you, this kind of intimacy is a love that cannot be matched-up. God's love is incomparable to *anything* or *anyone* on this earth.

WALK ON WATER

"Meanwhile, the boat was far out to sea when the wind came up against them and they were battered by the waves. At about four o'clock in the morning, Jesus came toward them walking on the water. They were scared out of their wits. 'A ghost!' they said, crying out in terror. But Jesus was quick to comfort them. 'Courage, it's me. Don't be afraid.' Peter, suddenly bold, said, 'Master, if it's really you, call me to come to you on the water.' He said, 'Come ahead.' Jumping out of the boat, Peter walked on the water to Jesus. But when he looked down at the waves churning beneath his feet, he lost his nerve and started to sink. He cried, 'Master, save me!' Jesus didn't hesitate. He reached down and grabbed his hand. Then he said, 'Faint-heart, what got into you?'"
(Matthew 14:24-31, MSG)

Peter and the rest of the disciples were already in a vulnerable, helpless state. They were out in the middle of nowhere with no one to rescue them should anything go wrong. The wind was strong and the waves of the sea came crashing down over and over again. They became overwhelmed with feelings of anxiety, fear, and uncertainty. Their lack of faith increased their terror when when they saw Jesus walking on water, even accusing him of being a ghost!

Jesus appeared to them and comforted them. Yet still, Peter wanted *proof* that Jesus was present. When Jesus summoned him, by *faith*, Peter stepped out of the boat and began walking on water! Can you imagine?

It is only when Peter took his eyes off of Jesus and focused on the harsh environment around him that he began to sink. When he cried out to Jesus, Jesus didn't hesitate in extending his hand and saving him. However, Jesus questioned his faith, " Faint-heart, what got into you?". Secure through the wind, saved from the crashing waves, walked on water, and he *still* lacked faith in Jesus' ability to save.

Beloved, where is your faith today? Is it in the harsh winds and the monstrous seas of your life? Or is it in the faith that Jesus will comfort and save you as you walk through it?

Walking through circumstances that no one else has ever walked through before takes *great* faith! Taking risks in areas that no one else has ever risked before takes *great* faith! Trusting Jesus in the midst of frightening circumstances takes *great* faith!

We all have difficulty trusting when life becomes tumultuous. The harshness of life can be unpredictable. Devastating news can paralyze and terrorize us, causing us to take our eyes off of Jesus. Nonetheless, it is during these times that our true character and our true faith is revealed.

So today I encourage you to get out of that boat, trust Jesus every step of the way, and start walking on water!

A Call to Unworldliness

"Do not love *or* cherish the world or the things that are in the world. If anyone loves the world, love for the Father is not in him..."
(1 John 2:15, AMP)

The definition of *world* here is not in reference to people, nature, or any of God's creation; but the realm of sin which opposes the ways of God.

Believers often confuse the word, *"worldly"* into thinking that it refers to the color of your hair, your salary, the type of clothes you wear, or your car model. Although we all have a responsibility and an accountability to the Lord with what we do with our time, talents, and offerings; these things alone do *not* define whether or not someone is *worldly*.

Many well-versed Christians can beautifully quote the above scripture out of context, but verse 16 tells us what the definition of *worldliness* is, *"For all that is in the world—the lust of the flesh [craving for sensual gratification] and the lust of the eyes [greedy longings of the mind] and the pride of life [assurance in one's own resources or in the stability of earthly things]—these do not come from the Father but are from the world [itself]."*

Those are the things that are worldly. However somehow, believers have found ways to justify these type of worldly indulgences because they are the unseen hidden things of the heart. Nonetheless, it doesn't make one less worldly because these desires are a bit more difficult to see.

Worldliness has very little to do with what someone wears. It has very little to do with that person with all those tattoos- trying to express their uniqueness. Or the one with the blue hair who is trying to break out of a mold.

God has created each one of us uniquely and we all have our distinct struggles. Judgements often give the perception that an individual needs to hide their struggles. We often see this with the man behind the pulpit, the woman behind the piano, or the little old lady in the pew with her pearl necklace and earrings on. I don't know about you but I would find our Christian community rather boring if we all looked the same, talked the same, lived the same. We are called to conformity in Christ, *not* uniformity.

John explains that worldly desires (lust of the flesh, lust of the eyes, greed, pride of life, arrogance) does not compare with love for God. If we as believers cannot love the people that we see are different from us, then the Word says we are *liars* because we cannot love a God who we do not see (1 John 4:20).

A Christian void of worldliness is not the one who has a three-piece suit on, the right dress on, or every hair in place. A Christian void of worldliness is one that knows how to love others as Jesus does.

Against All Odds

> "But the leaders of the city of Succoth said to Gideon, 'Why should we give your soldiers something to eat? You haven't caught Zebah and Zalmunna yet.'... Gideon left the city of Succoth and went to the city of Penuel. He asked the men of Penuel for food, just as he had asked the men of Succoth. But the men of Penuel gave Gideon the same answer that the men of Succoth had given.... When Gideon came to the city of Succoth, he said to the men of that city, 'Here are Zebah and Zalmunna. You made fun of me by saying, 'Why should we give food to your tired soldiers? You have not caught Zebah and Zalmunna yet.'"
> (Judges 8:6, 8, 15, ERV)

Reading the book of Judges, we naturally expect to find leaders who are good, noble, and honorable men who lead by example. However, the opposite is true. The judges of Israel were flawed and reprobate leaders that held a poor example of upstanding moral, model citizens.

When God called Gideon to capture Zebah and Zalmunna, his army had already been vastly outnumbered. These two kings had already shown their mighty strength in battle by invading the land of Israel. Not only did Gideon have to overcome his own doubts, but he had to constantly and consistently overcome the doubts of those around him.

However the *good* news is that God kept His promise and gave Gideon victory over Israel's enemies. Gideon remained faithful to God no matter what his critics had to say. In battle he took on far greater odds than were realistic to mere mortal men.

From Gideon's example we can learn that no matter how great the odds are against us, God is faithful in carrying out the plan, purpose, and vision He has for our lives. Through the book of Judges, we can see how God uses ordinary (imperfect) people to accomplish His mighty plans through obedient people.

Gideon went from being a warrior in hiding, threshing wheat at the foot of a hill to overcoming the very enemy he was initially hiding from.

When God calls you to do something extraordinary for Him, don't be surprised if the naysayers begin to doubt your call and your vision. In fact, if your vision is *not* too big, then I would say it is a *good* vision, not necessarily a *God* vision. It is when our dreams seem too big for us to accomplish that God can truly get the greater glory because every man will see that the task was impossible with man, but possible with God.

Is there something you are fearful of or hiding from today? Is there a task that the Lord wants you to do that seems too impossible to tackle?

Today I encourage you to pray that the Lord will give you a vision for His plan and purpose for you. Be attentive with open ears, open eyes, and open hearts and watch God get the glory as He gives you the victory over something that seems far too great for you!

Resurrection Day

"But let me tell you something wonderful, a mystery I'll probably never fully understand. We're not all going to die—*but* we are all going to be changed. You hear a blast to end all blasts from a trumpet, and in the time that you look up and blink your eyes—it's over. On signal from that trumpet from heaven, the dead will be up and out of their graves, beyond the reach of death, never to die again. At the same moment and in the same way, we'll all be changed. In the resurrection scheme of things, this has to happen: everything perishable taken off the shelves and replaced by the imperishable, this mortal replaced by the immortal. Then the saying will come true: Death swallowed by triumphant Life! Who got the last word, oh, Death? Oh, Death, who's afraid of you now?

It was sin that made death so frightening and law-code guilt that gave sin its leverage, its destructive power. But now in a single victorious stroke of Life, all three—sin, guilt, death—are gone, the gift of our Master, Jesus Christ. Thank God!"
(1 Corinthians 15:51-57, MSG)

Christ's resurrection rests on the evidence of many eye-witnesses, including Paul himself, and is the cornerstone of the Gospel. Those who deny the resurrection, also deny Christ, and the consequence of that is eternity in hell.

However, Paul explained that Christians would not face death. When Christ returns, the dead in Christ will be raised first but then those believers that are still alive will be caught up to meet Him. Jesus Christ removed the sting of Death and resurrected many to life even while He was still here on earth.

When Jesus prayed, He called the dead man Lazarus out of the cave, and onto life.

When Jesus met up with a ruler who found his twelve year old daughter dead, He took the child by her hand, told her to *"arise"*, and she awoke from her "sleep".

On another account, Jesus stopped a funeral procession where He touched the coffin and commanded a widow's only son back to life (imagine the faces of the witnesses)!

However, the promise of a resurrected life is not for everyone. Those who do not believe in Jesus Christ and His resurrection cannot enter the Kingdom of Heaven. There is no justification, or salvation, if Christ had not risen. The proof of the resurrection is missing body of our resurrected Lord.

All who believe in Christ have hope in him as Redeemer, hope for redemption, and hope for salvation by Him. If there is no resurrection, our hope is confined only to this life.

Christians are hated and persecuted by many. But yet still, Christians can enjoy solid comforts amidst all our difficulties and trials, even in the times of the sharpest persecution. This gift is only for believers that have given their lives to Christ. Jesus gives us the promise of eternal life.

This truth is confirmed by Old Testament prophecies and many who have seen Christ after His resurrection. Those that are believers in Christ, believe that Jesus was crucified, buried, and rose again from the dead. *This is the substance of true Christianity.*

Letting Go of the Past

"But the Lord says,
'Do not cling to events of the past or dwell on what happened long ago.
Watch for the new thing I am going to do. It is happening
already—you can see it now! I will make a road through
the wilderness and give you streams of water there.
Even the wild animals will honor me; jackals and
ostriches will praise me when I make rivers flow in
the desert to give water to my chosen people.'"
(Isaiah 43:18-20, GNT)

Often times it can be difficult to let go of events that have happened to us in the past. We can easily become complacent and content in doing life like it has always been done. We are on "survival mode" and adapting to change can be extremely challenging. But God frequently brings us into change and new seasons, lovingly surprising us with little (and grand) miracles along the way.

As we enter into the new seasons of our life, let us pull out those storage boxes that are tucked away in the back of our closet or maybe in the garage or basement. It is time to pull out the *warmer* clothes in preparation for *cooler* climates or *cooler* clothes in preparation for *warmer* climates.

But how many of us aren't quite ready for the new seasons and changes of our lives? How many of us plainly just don't *feel* like cleaning out closets to make room for the new season *(even though admittedly there had been many days we complained that we were ready for cooler months because "it's way too hot" or warmer months because "it's way too cold")*. "Ready or not, change is coming! If we don't prepare for the change, we could very well be wearing parkas in the warmer months of our lives or bathing suits in the colder months of our lives.

Many of us are *still* clinging on to events or seasons of the past. Many of us are reluctant to change, are clinging on to bad break-ups, disappointment, failures or hurts. Beloved, if we don't let go of last seasons relationships or hurts, we will miss out on God's new season for our lives and if not properly prepared, we could eventually freeze to death! Our hearts will become cold, hardened and embittered. We will become sour and skeptical of any new opportunities or relationships God wants to bring into our lives. Get the picture?

So today I encourage you, take time to *"clean out your closets"*, let go of the past and embrace the *new season* God wants to put in your path. To have a life we have never had before, we have to make room for God to do things that have never been done before. As we clean out our emotional *"closets"*, we can then make room for God to put streams in the wilderness areas of our life and rivers in the dry places of our life.

Your Joy is Coming

"So you'll go out in joy, you'll be led into a whole and complete life. The mountains and hills will lead the parade, bursting with song. All the trees of the forest will join the procession, exuberant with applause. No more thistles, but giant sequoias, no more thorn bushes, but stately pines— Monuments to me, to God, living and lasting evidence of God." (Isaiah 55:12-13, MSG)

God's Word never fails to accomplish His purpose. The Hebrews viewed God's spoken word as having POWER. Their belief was that once words left the mouth of a speaker, it could not be revoked. When God's people respond to Him in obedience, they can experience the reward of that obedience (Leviticus 26).

Ever heard of the giant sequoias? The sequoias are the largest living thing *on the planet*. The oldest living sequoia was discovered across King's Canyon in the Sierra Nevadas. It is more than 275 feet high, has a base diameter of 102 feet, weighs approximately 2.7 million pounds and is estimated to be more than 2,200 years old!

When the National Park Service took over the care of King's Canyon Park in the 1800s, they worked hard to prevent forest fires and protect the marvelous trees. However, 100 years later, they discovered they were actually working *against* the sequoia, because the sequoia *needs* fire for the cone to open and the seeds to germinate.

Since the sequoia can withstand fire that consumes most other trees, it is left standing after the fire is extinguished. As a result, the ground around it is not only cleared for its seeds to germinate, but the ground has also been fertilized with the ashes of those other burned trees and underbrush. The seeds can only grow successfully in full sunlight, free from overshadowing vegetation.

Fire is a purifying process even in forests. What looks like a trial for the sequoia is in reality the process they need for future growth.

Have you gone through any fiery trials lately? Know that God is using it to *grow* you!

Whatever you have been through, know that God is purifying you and growing you so you will be able to withstand *whatever* comes your way. Whatever you have gone through or experienced in life, does not only impact you but those around you. Your sphere of influence is watching and waiting to see how you will handle the fiery trials that come your way. Will you rebel against God, going your own way? Or will you obey, even in the midst of the fire and see God's great reward?

Christians are God's monument and we are to be evidence to the world of His existence. How are you handling your fiery trials today? Do not lose heart, joy is coming!

THE HEART-SHATTERED LIFE

> "Going through the motions doesn't please you, a flawless performance is nothing to you. I learned God-worship when my pride was shattered. Heart-shattered lives ready for love don't for a moment escape God's notice."
> (Psalm 51:16-17, MSG)

David had written this Psalm after he was confronted about having an affair with Bathsheba. He was feeling exposed, ashamed, humbled, and remorseful. Although David was a man after God's own heart (1 Sam 13:14), he acted absolutely contrary to what God desires and to what God had been teaching him throughout all his years. Interestingly David recognizes, *"Against you, you only have I sinned and done evil in your sight..."* (Psalm 51:4).

If God alone is the plumb-line, why then as Christians are we so readily available to persecute and condemn others when they fall short or sin (as if they have sinned against us personally)? God alone is the maker and ruler of the Law. If and *when* we sin, it is against God alone that we sin because next to His purity and holiness, the sin is exposed!

We have somehow embraced the false ideology that the more bible studies and church services we attend, the more "holy" we have become. This is not so! Works doesn't save us... Jesus does. However, when we are focusing on Jesus, *HE* will direct our paths on how to serve Him and it will not feel like works at all because it is done out of love... *not* obligation.

Our works are nothing but dirty rags to the Lord (Isaiah 64:6). God sees the motives and intentions of our heart. What pleases God more than works and sacrifices is a broken, humble spirit and a contrite heart. A heart that humbly recognizes that it falls short, doesn't have room to boast in its own performance while it belittles the performance of others.

When we as Believers do not truly understand God's salvation, His redemption, His love, and His forgiveness, *that* is when we as Believers exhaustingly try to "prove" to ourselves, God, and others that we are worthy. The result is simply, well, a worn-out Christian.

So where does the plumb-line lie? Well, God is the divine standard, the builder of His people, *He* tests and judges us. And He is ready and willing to forgive and rebuild his people. Shouldn't we as Christians do the same? Forgive and help rebuild God's people?

Today I encourage you to make yourself readily available for someone who has a fallen, sinful, prideful, heart-shattered life. There may be someone that crosses your path that is waiting and willing to embrace God's unfailing love through *you*.

When Evil Prevails

"Jerusalem is doomed, that corrupt, rebellious city that oppresses its own people. It has not listened to the Lord or accepted his discipline. It has not put its trust in the Lord or asked for his help. Its officials are like roaring lions; its judges are like hungry wolves, too greedy to leave a bone until morning. The prophets are irresponsible and treacherous; the priests defile what is sacred, and twist the law of God to their own advantage. But the Lord is still in the city; he does what is right and never what is wrong. Every morning without fail, he brings justice to his people. And yet the unrighteous people there keep on doing wrong and are not ashamed."
(Zephaniah 3:1-5, GNT)

We all wrestle with the difficult age-old questions, *"Why do the wicked prosper?"* and *"Why do the righteous suffer?"* It is especially difficult when you feel you have done right by God and experience hardship, while the person next to you has little to no regard for God and seemingly gets ahead. You have been exasperated praying and believing God for His promises, but things in your life have not turned out as you had hoped. It may seem as if God doesn't even hear your prayers anymore. But the guy who scoffs at God appears to be doing great. You begin to wonder, *"Why follow God when all I get is trials? If there is a God of justice in Heaven, why doesn't He do something about all the injustice in the world? Is it worth it to follow the Lord?"*

In the Bible, we see several examples of God's people struggling with this same questions. Many of their enemies were godless and yet seemed to prosper. Many Believers had become disappointed with God. He had not done for them what they had hoped. But God has a plan to right every wrong and punish all evildoers. If we are not living right by God, we will be terrified at Jesus' second coming.

Officials... rulers... prophets... priests were all classes of leaders that were reprimanded for indulging in a conduct that was completely opposed to their calling and their responsibilities. These *treacherous* people were claiming to be people of God but only proclaimed lies. They violated God's Law when they were supposed to be teachers *of* the Law.

The above scripture is not a "feel good" scripture. We could easily accuse Zephaniah of being a "doomsday prepper". But the reality is, the prophet's purpose for such harsh words was to bring God's people to repentance and instill future hope.

Zephaniah describes a coming Great Day of the Lord that is fast approaching (Zeph 1:1-2:3). While initially Zephaniah bluntly warns his listeners to expect judgement, he also reaffirms God's lasting love for His own. There will always be consequences for sin, but God is committed to saving His people until the end. As God reminds us in Zephaniah 3:17...

> "The Lord your God is with you;
> his power gives you victory.
> The Lord will take delight in you,
> and in his love he will give you new life.
> He will sing and be joyful over you."

Cross-Gender Boundaries

"Now Joseph was well-built and handsome, and after a while his master's wife took notice of Joseph and said, 'Come to bed with me!' But he refused. 'With me in charge,' he told her, 'my master does not concern himself with anything in the house; everything he owns he has entrusted to my care. No one is greater in this house than I am. My master has withheld nothing from me except you, because you are his wife. How then could I do such a wicked thing and sin against God?' And though she spoke to Joseph day after day, he refused to go to bed with her or even be with her. But one day when Joseph went into the house to do his work, none of the house servants was there. She caught him by his robe and said, 'Come to bed with me.' But he escaped and ran outside, leaving his robe in her hand."
(Genesis 39:6-12)

Read the books, read the articles, watch the news and most often than not, you will hear *some* story of someone being caught in the act of adultery. We are living in a day and age where sexual perversion is rampant and we are in an *all-out-war* for the sanctity and purity of marriage.

Perhaps you are thinking, *"This can't be a problem in the church. No way! Certainly the moral standards of Christians are much higher!"* Most Christians foolishly believe that they are exempt from this type of temptation or that this could never happen to a man or woman "of the cloth". But *"pride comes before the fall"* (Proverbs 16:18).

Christianity Today did a study and found that 45 percent of its subscribers indicated having done something inappropriate with someone of the opposite sex. These are shocking statistics, especially while considering that *Christianity Today* readers tend to be college-educated church leaders, elders, deacons, Sunday school superintendents, and teachers! If this is for the Church's leadership, how much more temptation for the average member of the congregation? Only God knows! However, there is *growing* evidence that adultery is a tremendous problem in Christian circles.

I have been utterly amazed to see how many Christians think *nothing* of having a private lunch, face-booking, emailing, texting, or messaging someone of the opposite sex. When men and women do this, they are opening themselves up for temptation. They will *surely* fall.

Women tend to bear the brunt of this negative approach, often being called a *"Jezebel"* or mistakingly taking friendliness for flirtation. But men do not fare well either. Either way, men and women must be honest about their fallen desires and act appropriately to avoid them. They must refrain from any hint of evil, refusing to engage in any one on one relationships with someone of the opposite sex.

Notice, Joseph *ran* from the tempting woman. He didn't dabble on facebook, he didn't send her a sweet text, he didn't send her an email with a bunch of smiley faces on it, and he *certainly* didn't have a private lunch or dinner with her! Men and women of God often do this and justify their actions by spiritualizing it. They often think it obviates them from temptation but indeed it does not! All in all, avoiding crossing gender boundaries can become a slippery slope.

So what do we do in a world where interfacing with the opposite sex is inevitable? Should we all wear parkas and hang our heads low, avoiding all possible eye-contact? Of course not! But we *are* to be mindful of such things and go the extra mile to uphold certain boundaries and standards. As Christians, *we* have the responsibility of not giving the enemy a foothold and being mindful of temptations that linger.

Joseph made the right decision when dealing with Potiphar's wife. His reaction to her advances was one of the utmost integrity, holding up God's standards in the face of temptation.

Today I urge you to carry out healthy boundaries when it comes to those of the opposite sex. No matter their title or position, if temptation comes knocking at your door, I pray that you will be a person of utmost integrity and uphold God's standards, just as Joseph did.

BE SET FREE

> "He [Pharaoh] called for Moses and Aaron by night, and
> said, 'Rise up, get out from among my people, both you
> and the Israelites; and go, serve the Lord, as you said.
> Also take your flocks and your herds, as you have said,
> and be gone! And [ask your God to] bless me also.'"
> (Exodus 12:31-32, AMP)

Pharaoh was the most powerful person in ancient Egypt. He was rich and famous throughout the land although he lived a lifestyle of every kind of immorality. He was the political and religious leader of the Egyptian people, holding many "titles". He built many pyramids and statues in his image and was considered a "god" in Egypt.

Although Pharaoh had previously sworn that he never wanted to see Moses' face again (10:28), it was *Pharaoh* who requested a *face to face* meeting with Moses. After experiencing many plagues and much tragedy and turmoil, Pharaoh finally agreed to let God's people go. Even adding, "... *ask your God to bless me also*". It was his final admittance of defeat and his confession that Moses' God was who He said He was.

The Lord's care for His people is sovereign over all the earth (as displayed through the plagues that brought their deliverance). Lofty Pharaoh had a hardened heart and wanted to keep God's people enslaved and in bondage. He finally came to the realization that Egypt's standards were inadequate in comparison to the Lord's righteous standards.

Many of us have been "let go" from the past Pharoah's in our life. Maybe it was in the form of broken relationships, the loss of a loved one, lost dreams, broken finances, failure in a career, at a church, or the like. Maybe that *was* a tragic experience. But maybe now God has set you free with *new* relationships, a *new* career path, *new* finances, *new* fellowship, a *new* life! But sadly, many of us are still walking around like we are in *bondage*... the past pains engraved in our hearts and minds... still fresh... still carrying all those chains and shackles of past tragedies.

God is not unjust. He reveals His patience even for those that deserve punishment. My prayer for you is that you will have intimate knowledge of the freedom that comes with Jesus' crucification on the cross. My prayer is that you will no longer live a life of bondage when God died to set us free. May you walk in His glorious presence and seek HIS truth that the truth may set you free! He will use *every* situation in your life to make known His righteousness, saving power, and brilliant glory.

Are You Running the Right Race?

"We are assured *and* know that [God being a partner in their labor] all things work together *and* are [fitting into a plan] for good to *and* for those who love God and are called according to [His] design *and* purpose. For those whom He foreknew [of whom He was aware and loved beforehand], He also destined from the beginning [foreordaining them] to be molded into the image of His Son [and share inwardly His likeness], that He might become the firstborn among many brethren.
(Romans 8:28-29, AMP)

God loved us and purposed a destiny for us before we had any knowledge of Him. He knew us before the foundations of the earth. In the beginning He called us by name and set out a purpose for us. He didn't *"hang us out to dry"* but instead, decreed our lives with a specific intention and fate. Can you fathom it? Now that's something worth celebrating!

Most of us can easily forget that there is a perfect plan for our lives. We like to be in control of *all* aspects of our lives. Giving up control leaves us feeling too vulnerable. We'd like to think we know it all too(try discussing theology with individuals from different denominations). It's good to have purpose, meaning, and goals for our lives, but not to the point where we become so self-absorbed, we trample on people along the way.

Someone who struggles with letting go of control exude signs of deep-seeded issues. They typically suffer from feelings of insecurity, codependency, fear, anxiety and are distrustful with people and most importantly, are distrustful with giving God supreme rule over their lives.

The truth is, as much as we would like to think we have it all together and want to control *everything,* there are many things we cannot control.

That job we didn't get, that horrible rumor spread about us, disease, that unwanted divorce, sickness, death, etc. *A lot* of things our out of our control. That's how God designed it so we would learn to rely solely on *Him*. At the point where we let go of control, we can allow God to take the reigns and lead us into His perfect plan for our lives. There is so much peace, rest, and freedom that comes with letting go!

So many Believers live a life of bondage coping with fear, anxiety, and restlessness... striving earnestly to "make things happen" for *themselves*. When you begin to hand control over to God, you will experience amazing joy in your life knowing that no matter what, God's got your back. You will no longer find it a vulnerability to remove the mask of unwanted expectations. The enemy tries to keep God's people in bondage by deceiving us into thinking we have to meet unrealistic expectations (from ourselves or others) that ultimately only leads to unfulfillment. Think about it. How many of us have said, "When I get married.... when I have the right job.... make more money... have the right car... when I retire... find the right church... have a child... have *three* children... get a promotion... when I graduate... when I lose weight... *then* I will be happy." Only to find that the *"thing"* waiting on the other side never truly satisfied and repetitiously, we move on over to the next *"want"*.

Sadly, Christian's skewed view of "theology" mixed with the world's demands has led many Believers to live an unsatisfied unfulfilled life. The lie that we are not good enough until we *(you fill in the blank)*... has led many Christian's to tirelessly run the wrong race. The only race God is calling us to run is not one of this world's system, but one that keeps the faith (2 Timothy 4:7). God promises to, "...work all things together for the good of those who love Him and are called according to his purpose." Understanding this, letting go of control and trusting God is where genuine freedom, joy, and contentment resides.

THE TIME IS RIPE FOR A MIRACLE

"As He went on His way to Jerusalem, it occurred that [Jesus] was passing [along the border] between Samaria and Galilee. And as He was going into one village, He was met by ten lepers, who stood at a distance. And they raised up their voices and called, 'Jesus, Master, take pity *and* have mercy on us!' And when He saw them, He said to them, 'Go [at once] and show yourselves to the priests'. And as they went, they were cured *and* made clean. Then one of them, upon seeing that he was cured, turned back, recognizing *and* thanking *and* praising God with a loud voice; And he fell prostrate at Jesus' feet, thanking Him [over and over]. And he was a Samaritan. Then Jesus asked, 'Were not [all] ten cleansed? Where are the nine? Was there no one found to return and to recognize *and* give thanks *and* praise to God except this alien?' And He said to him, 'Get up and go on your way. Your faith (your trust and confidence that spring from your belief in God) has restored you to health.'"
(Luke 17:11-19, AMP)

Leprosy was a horrific disease that repulsed and terrified all who came in contact with it. It was incurable by human means, it was isolating *(lepers were confined outside the city limits - many times to the city dump where they could scavenge for food and other things)*, and it would cause one to become ceremonially unclean if in contact with a leper *(even if you didn't specifically catch this disease)*. Understandably, this often left lepers feeling lonely, rejected, feared, and outcasted.

Samaria was considered to be a land defiled and forsaken by God. Thus, Samaritans, just like the lepers, were *also* outcasted – particularly by the Galileans. Samaria was considered the land of "sinners" and no one dared go near it (or *them*). Yet still, as God would have it, it was the place the Son of God visited and performed one of His greatest miracles. Isn't just like God to *want* people that are *unwanted* by so many? God has a way of turning our idiosyncrasies of society upside down. I find it interesting that God would choose to heal a *leprous* Samaritan. I mean we are talking the worst of the worst here... as if being a *Samaritan* (illegal alien) wasn't enough, he then had to be a leprous one!

Galilee was the land where the rational, the proud, and the intellectual resided. The Lord had already had an unpleasant experience there because He was "just the Son of a Carpenter" and often looked down upon. Galilee was the place where pride prevailed over conviction, and where Jesus had been refused the most.

The book of Luke was particularly interested in showing Jesus' concern for the oppressed and the poor.

Sometimes it is during the dark times of oppression and opposition that God performs His greatest miracle. Only one of the ten lepers, a *Samaritan*, returned to thank Jesus. Jesus was no doubt, grieved over the ingratitude of the other nine lepers.

I wonder if anyone reading this has ever felt like a "leper". Maybe going through an obstacle, sickness, or disease that has left you feeling oppressed. Maybe you feel hopeless and see no way out of your present situation or circumstance. Maybe you have felt shunned by society, your family, or worse... your church. Maybe at times, you feeling rejected and repulsed by everyone in society. Well I am here to tell you that the time is *ripe* for a miracle in your life. Hold fast and do not give up! When God brings you through (and He *will* bring you through), do not forget to go back and *thank* Him. Better yet, start praising Him and thanking Him *now* for the miracle He is about to do in your life.

Kicking Over the Money Tables

"Jesus went straight to the Temple and threw out everyone who had set up shop, buying and selling. He kicked over the tables of loan sharks and the stalls of dove merchants. He quoted this text:

'My house was designated a house of prayer;
You have made it a hangout for thieves.'
Now there was room for the blind and crippled to get in. They came to Jesus and he healed them." (Matthew 21:12-14, MSG)

God's action teaches us that if believers are deceitful or use the church for the wrong reason, there will be dire consequences. Religious authorities allowed money-changers and sellers inside the outer court of the temple. Believers bought all sorts of merchandise in exchange for money that was acceptable to religious leaders.

These temple-sanctioned businesspeople were inside a place of worship. They viewed people in the congregation as a means to make a "buck". When people profane sacred things by trying to profit financially from them, they become hindered to the sensitivity to God's spirit. Their church vision becomes skewed, eyes become clouded by the almighty dollar, and individuals are viewed as financial opportunities versus precious people of God that need ministering to. The problem only intensifies when this mindset is being fulfilled by church leaders.

Jesus drove these church leaders out because he didn't want the house of his father to become a house of merchandise.

Financial opportunist make it difficult for common people to worship God. Everyone becomes money-driven versus soul-driven.

When we come to worship God, we must put aside all distractions and agendas. Jesus wants his people to experience the joy and peace of undistracted devotion to him.

Today, many ambitious church leaders are still persuading parishioners to give excessively while promising a huge return on their investment. Greed can lead the church's "businessman" to be quite persuasive, but make no mistake, this is often done out of selfish gains and investments. Church members with larger financial statements are given preferential treatment over the poor, the widow, or the orphan. Misappropriation of funds can quickly be determined by how the needy are cared for within the church. If the "less fortunate" are often ignored, then this is evidence that something is amiss.

We all have an accountability to The Lord when it comes to how we handle finances. So the next time a businessman, church leader, or your pastor wants to see your financial statement; remind him that your heart (and your finances) remains in the hands of God.

MENDING BROKEN HEARTS

"My sacrifice, O God, is a broken spirit;
a broken and contrite heart you, God, will
not despise." (Psalm 51:17, NIV)

What pleases god more than sacrifice is a humble heart that looks to Him in times of trouble. Heartache is one of the most painful things an individual can experience. Albeit from a loss of a loved one, sin, broken relationships, or broken dreams. The hopes of "happily ever after" often seem to crumble. Being honest with God in the midst of brokenness, helps us to find our way back into His presence.

David reminds us that the only path to forgiveness is a broken heart and a humble spirit. When we humble ourselves before the mercy of God, He delights to lift us up (Luke 18:13-14). When we openly acknowledge our sin against God, turn from it, and cry out for cleansing, God promises that He will hear us and forgive (1 John 1:9). A broken spirit and a contrite heart invites God to clean us and restore us to right relationship back to Him.

Often our own fleshly desires clouds the perfect desires God has for our lives. It is only through true repentance and surrender that we can see the Son shine on our lives once again.

Sometimes it is through our brokenness that God can awaken us unto Himself and redirect our paths towards Him. Turning to God in the midst of loss is our only hope for total restoration.

After turning to God's mercy, and then praying for forgiveness and cleansing, we can then begin the path God's renewal and sustainability for our lives. We become passionately committed to being changed by God.

The Lord accepts and forgives those who are honest with Him, who are humble before Him, and who recognize their dependence on God's grace.

Being a Christian does not mean that we are beyond brokenness in this life. Unless we are content in the very sin that destroys us, seasons of brokenness will be evident in our lives until The Lord takes us home.

Maybe you are searching and cannot find any sin in your heart today. Maybe you cannot relate to the sins of David. Yet still, no matter the reason for your brokenness, it does not go unseen by God and He is ready and willing to heal your heart. God alone is the mender of broken hearts!

Printed in the United States
By Bookmasters